HEALING DIVISION
How Balancing Empathy and Power Can Heal American Society

By Amy E. Hull, M.Ed.

First paperback edition November 2025

Cover and Interior Design by Heather Seeger
Illustrations copyright © 2025 by Wayfinding, LLC

ISBN: 978-1-955051-47-7 (Hardback)
ISBN: 978-1-955051-48-4 (Paperback)
ISBN: 978-1-955051-49-1 (e-Book)

Published in association with Punchline Publishers
www.punchlineagency.com

www.amyehull.com
Facebook: Amy E. Hull Official
Instagram: @amyehull_official
Twitter/X: @theamyehull

TABLE OF CONTENTS

DEDICATION:

For My Family - your legacy of unconditional love and resilience supports me.

For My Boys, My Greatest Gifts - the desire to continue the family legacy for you motivates me every minute, every hour, every day.

INTRODUCTION

The concept for this book is a result of the lifelong work I have done as a scientist, educator, and executive leader. My father taught my sister and I many life lessons, but one in particular involved hard work and caring for others: he ensured that we always worked some sort of job from the second we were able to earn a wage. He was also clear that service to others and building relationships with others were key to success. My first job was a babysitter. I have always loved taking care of kids, even when I was a kid myself, so it made sense that this was my first job. You will learn more about this in the opening chapter.

By the time I had graduated from college, I had worked as: a cashier for Blockbuster Video, telemarketer, a package sorter at the post-office bulk mail center during the holiday season, a retail cashier and floor assistant, an intern in emergency medicine at a local children's hospital, a part-time singer at a local church, and a receptionist at a popular salon and day spa. After graduating from college, I was a lab technician completing research on sickle cell anemia and T-cell leukemia at one of the best children's hospitals in the world. I was a graduate assistant in the Office of Student Affairs while getting my master's degree. I became a certified wedding planner, coordinating several weddings, including my own, and then found my lifelong career when I finished my certification and master's degree in secondary education and became an educator.

For seventeen years as an educator, my real understanding of the complexities of empathy and power dynamics became more apparent and real.

Several years into my career as an educator, I got divorced and learned how to balance up to three jobs at once while learning how to best co-parent as a new single adult at the same time. While working as a full-time high school assistant principal with two kids who were two and six years old, I took on a part-time position at DSW shoe store (and selfishly, the shoe discounts were a great perk), and was a karaoke DJ at a local bar and grill on Friday nights for three years. That time in my life was humbling, but also offered a perspective that I didn't have while married. I grew in my empathy and understanding of those who were just trying to survive and do the best that they can for their families.

I also realized during this time that my career in education as a teacher and administrator, and the passion I had for helping people, centered on educating others about historically marginalized communities and valuing and celebrating *all* people—their cultures, their history, and their place in the world. This prompted me to start my own consulting business while I was an educator in 2018, in which I consulted several different business teams and schools in leadership development, coaching and feedback, interpersonal communication strategy, training, emotional intelligence, and more. I continued volunteering and started serving on non-profit boards and leadership teams. This portion of my career in education showed me what happens when empathy and power are in balance (or not) with one another in businesses, communities, local government, society, and organizational systems, the bureaucracy of public education, and how an imbalance often results in a divisive and unacceptable environment in which children must grow up.

The COVID-19 pandemic brought another complicated level of empathy and power imbalances in which the call for basic human care and compassion for others took the main stage. And while we saw several instances of empathy across the country, we also witnessed brutal abuse of power at the same time, resulting in the deaths of so many who were not provided the access or empathy needed in order to survive.

My latest observations of imbalances in empathy and power came when I entered Corporate America in late 2020 as a leader in human resources. I built an entire department of an organization from the ground up and worked to become an executive, reporting directly to the Chief Human Resources Officer. Since then, I have worked on teams and experienced the excitement when the company acquired other businesses, and also experienced the unknowns and feelings of uncertainty as an employee of a business that was acquired. This for-profit business world provided me with an enormous amount of learning, perspective, and opportunity for my career and my family, and also a close-up view of what power looks like in a corporate environment.

I have experienced highs in this field, like when I was invited to join business leaders and ring the bell on Wall Street at NASDAQ when the company became a publicly traded entity, to lows, like when I sat hoping I would still have a role at our company when we were acquired. I have witnessed and navigated times of change for several different workforce populations, whether students, adults, community members, or employees, over the last twenty-five years of work.

I have traveled to twenty-seven states (I really need to get to the middle of the U.S.) and eleven countries. I would never claim to be all-knowing, but through my studies, lived experiences, and professional experiences, I have led individuals, teams, and businesses in what it means to introduce balances of empathy and power into the work environment.

Research and contributions for this book were born out of the culmination of all of the learning I have done throughout my studies, observations from lived personal and professional experiences, and developing strategies for educators and leaders across job sectors, levels, and industries. For you, I have put all this information into one place that explains empathy and power dynamics and how they show up in others and create division across America.

Division and separation are perpetuated by those in power for several reasons, and when there is an imbalance of empathy and power or misuse of power, division is maintained. This, I will argue, is the root cause of the societal issues in America.

Societal issues like racism, sexism, homophobia, transphobia, economic inequalities, poverty, a lack of access to healthcare and affordable housing, a diminished focus on mental health, and more are all examples and results of empathy and power imbalances. These issues are a result of a person or a group of people in positions of power who exert power over others who are at risk or less privileged. When there isn't an adequate balance of empathy to ensure that people across America remain supported, in community with one another, and at peace, we experience division and imbalance.

These societal issues are *symptoms* of the imbalance and represent what becomes a dichotomous way of thinking at both the macro and micro levels of our country. I use the word dichotomous because people are forced into thinking that they must choose a side on every issue rather than being taught that more than one thing can be true at the same time. In other words, they don't learn how to balance empathy and power for a peaceful and unified solution that encompasses a multitude of combined perspectives and experiences.

Misusing power is a significant mechanism of creating division. If someone in a position of power and authority abuses that power or perpetuates the idea that there is only one option in every scenario, it will greatly influence and pressure people to make a choice, thereby naturally causing an either/or mindset. This divisive mindset leads people to be judgmental, rigid, and closed off to the acceptance of how others live.

In the following chapters, I detail empathy and how it appears in everyday life, share research about 36 types of power, and give real-life stories and scenarios to help you visualize and apply a balance of empathy and power using the Balance B.L.U.E.Print©. I'll present some self-investigative activities and share exactly what happens when empathy and power are imbalanced in several different areas of life and work. Most importantly, I'll explain how to recognize these imbalances in ourselves, our teams, our community, or wherever we are. We can have a balanced society where power still exists and works in tandem with empathetic leadership.

The outcome of this balance is the healing of division and bringing our society into a balanced, empathetic and powerful place for all.

CHAPTER 1:
The Situation Room

Growing up, I always had my sights set on becoming a doctor. I wanted to be a pediatrician with an intensity so strong I could feel it in the pit of my stomach. Imagining myself in a white coat, examining and holding all the adorable babies mad me so excited! I was so invested that even as a young child in kindergarten, my mom and dad quickly discovered my dream job.

For Christmas that year, my parents did what every parent in the early '90s did for their young daughters, and they scavenged the toy stores for a Cabbage Patch Doll to gift me. Let me tell you, though, it was not just ANY Cabbage Patch Doll, but the *preemie* Cabbage Patch Doll, because they knew I loved little babies. On top of that, they got me the Cabbage Patch diapers so I could pretend I had a real little baby to look after and take care of. What they didn't realize is that even in my little six-year-old brain, I was ready to give my little preemie a medical problem, and in the span of five minutes, I opened and used every single diaper. The way my mom tells it, I walked right into the kitchen where she thought she had bought herself some alone time to get dinner ready, and I looked at her and said, "She won't stop peeing!" My mom, who eventually became a preschool teacher, looked at me calmly and said, "What do you mean, Amy?"

Apparently, with more force, I said, "She WON'T STOP PEEING!" We went to the living room where she found every single diaper "used," and unable to be reused (in that day, the diapers were *not* resealable).

As a parent of my own now, I'm frustrated recalling that memory because I'm sure my parents searched high and low for that doll, and God only knows how much they paid for the preemie diapers to be gone in less than five minutes. I had given my little preemie a urinary problem, and I was only six. That is how my journey into pre-medicine started, but after four years of college as a pre-med biology major, the journey abruptly ended. I told my parents just three days before I was supposed to take the MCAT (the medical school entrance exam) that I decided NOT to go to medical school and was changing career paths altogether: I wanted to be a science teacher. In my Junior year I got to teach a supplemental Biology class to non-major students taking Biology and the immediate joy of impacting another person directly challenged me to change my career aspirations.

Once I graduated from college, I took a year to be solid in my decision and then received my Masters degree and certification to teach. I taught life sciences to junior high and high school students. You know, everyone's favorite subjects in school: biology, earth, physical, and environmental science (cue the sarcasm, although I think my students loved me, if I do say so myself). I made a mantra for the students that had me as their teacher: I would be fun, fair, and we would have a good time, but the class would not be an easy way through. I wanted them to know they could approach me with anything, that all students were accepted, and that they could be themselves with me, but this didn't mean they wouldn't learn or not have to work hard. And it worked! I still have connections to some of my students from over seventeen years ago.

About halfway through my teaching career, I started to get comfortable with my practice. They say it takes about five years to really feel like you have a handle on things. Just as I started to hit that five year goal, and true to form for me, I eventually started to feel boxed in, like my entire career life was the same thing over and over again, year after year, with little variety. Lesson planning, curriculum, textbook reviews, Microsoft Word, Excel, and minimal PowerPoint, overhead projector notes, grading, teacher conferences day in and day out—the same old same old. Not to mention, my classroom was an inside room with a back door and no windows, so I also felt like I was in a box all day long.

Eventually, my mom asked me, "Why don't you consider becoming an assistant principal? Go into administration!" At this point, she was an elementary school principal in a Montessori program school. I looked at her like she had lost her ever-loving mind. In fact, I remember laughing like she had just told the best joke since Richard Pryor, and I remember saying something along the lines of, "You must be crazy! Ain't no way! Why would I want to do something like THAT?!"

After weeks of talking and persuasion, she convinced me to attend an informational session about a master's degree program at one of the local universities that was built for current professionals to obtain their certification in administration and a master's degree at the same time in one full year. Full-time. I was married then, with a 20-month-old, and teaching full-time. But my crazy self went and did it anyway.

After graduation, it came time for me to start applying for potential positions at the schools in the city. The most obvious choice was the school district where I was already a teacher. I already had a few conversations with my current building principal (who happened to be my administrative mentor in my program and would become a great future mentor in my professional career) about potential openings in other schools in the district. One school in our district, where I had shadow experience, was very interested in me as the application period slowly approached.

Like I mentioned before, my mom was an elementary school principal in the same district at the time, and my dad had served on the school district board while I was a high school student. One of the greatest days of my life was the day I graduated high school, because he was president of the school board that year and was the district representative on stage. My dad got to give me my high school diploma, along with all of my friends. It was amazing and I knew how special and unique it was to get that opportunity. He was well-known in the educator circuit at the time.

So, here we are. In all, there were dozens of schools within my district. The application process opened, and I knew with certainty that I would be a great candidate. I had teaching experience in one of the best public high schools in the state (and even the country, for that matter), and I had great recommendations and did very well in my master's program.

After I applied, I started noticing that some other applicants were announcing their school assignments. In my region of public schools, a person "works at the pleasure of the superintendent," which means you do not work or interview for an individual school, per se, you apply and interview for any school opening in that district. If someone is hired as a new assistant principal, senior leaders in the district place the newly hired administrator in a school of their choice with an opening. Rarely do newly hired assistant principals get a choice of where they work in their first year. Where you end up is the decision of the senior leaders in the district. It was mid-summer, I didn't have a position yet, and I was getting nervous that the district would not offer me an opportunity to interview for an open role as an assistant principal.

In mid-July, my chance finally came in the form of a phone call to interview in the district. I was very excited! I talked to my mom, who knew the ins and outs of the district from her experience as an elementary principal, and began networking with several others. I learned that there were only two more open assistant principal positions left for the following school year. I wondered why I didn't get an interview sooner when I knew I had the credentials. I learned that many positions were filled by other assistant principals in the district who were shifting between buildings. The two openings left in the district were located in urban city neighborhoods and what some on the outside might label an "inner city school." I was not intimidated by this, but it was vastly different from the school I had taught in for the previous seven years. Despite this, I remained confident.

On the day of my interview, I bought a new business outfit, a two-piece dress, and a suit jacket. It was sienna brown—not a dull brown, but like the color of the reddish clay dirt in the southern U.S. It had a one-inch ivory border around the sleeves and bottom of the dress. It was cute, but subtle. Neutral colors, of course, per the business etiquette before COVID-19 changed some of the allowances for what work attire can look like. I also had to make all of the consolations as a woman. Some of us know these well: not too much makeup, not too much overpowering aroma of perfume, not too nice, not too weak of a handshake, not too confident, but not too shy. Basically, it was a small version of the speech that America Ferrara gave in the hit movie, *Barbie*. I walked with my small leather brief (which belonged to my dad), which inside held my resume and notepad for taking notes, if any, during the interview, along with my pre-written reminders and questions. I was ready!

Or, so I thought.

Let me introduce you to: The Situation Interrogation Room, a.k.a. my interview room. Wolf Blitzer was not in the room, and neither was Olivia Benson (I love me some *Law & Order SVU*), but you could cut the energy and tension in my interview room with a knife. I was greeted by a current principal whom I knew, not well, but well enough to be cordial. She led me into the room, and I smiled and greeted everyone. There was a large oval shaped conference table with about ten people seated around it. Some smiled kindly, and a few did not change their facial expressions. The room was not brightly lit, but perhaps had some warm light, which made it feel like it might be dark outside. There were no windows in this room to the outside. Again—interrogation.

The interview started normally, but quickly I found that the tone of the questions changed from a polite inquiry about my experiences, such as "Tell us about your experience in your current role…" to much more specific and invasive, "How much do you know about the pyramid of interventions?"

I defined the pyramid of interventions, detailed who was served at each level, and provided an example of my use of it. Admittedly, I didn't have an extensive amount of experience executing strategies with students at *every* level of the pyramid because the school I had taught in had fewer students in the tier that required the most support for students, which was the opposite of the school where I was interviewing.

"So, you don't know anything about working with the bottom tier and how to serve those students?" As I looked around the room, I noticed that I was being judged and grilled. The faces looking back at me, especially by one person in particular, were now furrowed brows and doubt. In this one person, I saw confusion, almost as if it was incredulous that I had the audacity to be present in the room.

I had anticipated this.

Prior to the interview, I became aware of a rumor that I had only gotten the interview because of my parents and their previous experience in this school district. Also, this one person had an unpleasant encounter with my mom in years past. To me, this also explained why I was not one of the initial interviews for new hires in this district and interviewed when there were only two open positions remaining. Their line of questioning felt purposeful, as if to make me work harder to prove I was qualified enough to take on an administrative role and deserved an interview. Despite my years as a successful teacher, finishing my program with a 4.0 GPA, passing all certification tests, and getting high recommendations from my administrative shadow experiences, it was clear that some believed I was only there because of my parents.

Here is where it got real—really bad, I should say. It was a *tiny* bit my fault for responding to their question with an emotionally charged answer, but I also felt defensive of who I was, rather than being invited to show all that I was and what I could do in the role.

The next question I received came from the one person who I could tell had already made up their mind about me before I even walked into the room. She asked me, "What makes you think *you* could be successful at a school like this when you have never taught at a school like this or, by your own words, know how to work the pyramid of interventions?"

I am no interview expert now, and I definitely wasn't then, but what I can tell you is that there was nothing empathetic, calm, inviting, or equitable about her tone. I definitely knew that those types of questions would not get the best of someone in an interview, and it was not the proper way to ask a question in one, either.

So, knowing what I knew about my reputation, I responded with a prepared answer. What I didn't anticipate was the accompanying emotions that poured out after being interrogated for a full thirty-five minutes and then receiving such a direct, and what felt like hostile, question. My emotions were running high.

I responded, "Because any job I have had, I have completed successfully. In my teaching roles, students learn successfully, and professionally I advance in leadership. I work hard. I never do anything halfway. My dad taught us to..."

And that was when I felt the tears welling and my throat tightening to try and hold it all back. But I couldn't. The passion I felt for my field, plus mentioning my dad, was a formula for overflow.

You see, my dad had passed away not exceptionally long before my interview, and the wound was still fresh as I brought him up, combined with the tension and pressure I felt during the interview. Crying was the worst thing that could have happened at that moment. I actually heard the person who asked the question say, "Is she for real crying right now?" very softly but definitely audibly.

I quickly apologized for the reaction, and I knew I needed a second to calm down and continue. It was supremely embarrassing, but also a product of being interrogated rather than made to feel I was in a safe space. I felt like some of my interviewers were exerting an unhealthy power dynamic over me because they were feeling powerful in that moment to put me in a place they wanted me to be, instead of being empathetic and seeing me for my successful reputation rather than assuming my parents were the only reason I was there.

Several people at the table knew the influence my dad had in our city and about his recent passing.

One person interjected, "Let's take five and come back."

I stepped out and entered another room, where another interviewer came in to ensure I was okay.

I replied, "Yes, it's just embarrassing. I did not want that to happen and detract from what I'm capable of, and now it appears to everyone that I'm weak and won't be able to handle myself in this role."

After returning, there were some additional questions, but I couldn't even tell you what they were at this point. In my mind, I had ruined my chances at an assistant principal role while, at the same time, I was seething mad at how the interview had gone down.

I immediately called my mom when I left the interview, who joined me in being livid about the interviewer, and I told her that I was pretty sure I wouldn't get a position.

She was optimistic, "You don't know that. There were other people in the room who may have understood. Just give it time and go talk to your principal mentor." So that's what I did. I slept on it and then decided to speak to my principal mentor the next day.

My principal mentor beat me to it and stopped by my classroom the following day, asking if I could chat after school about the interview. He said he wanted to "get my take on what occurred." I could tell from his tone and his approach that it was more out of inquiry based on a conversation he may have had with someone in that Situation Interrogation Room. I just didn't know who. As I went through my day, I overthought the entire scenario and convinced myself that they tasked my mentor with telling me I was out.

At the end of the day, I entered his office. He slightly grinned and asked how the teaching day went with "the kids." I sat down, and we engaged in some small educational talk, and then he asked about the previous day.

"So, what happened yesterday? I gotta tell ya, I got a call, and I was a little taken aback, so I wanted to hear from your perspective what happened."

I knew I could speak freely and confidentially with him about my experience, and at the end of it, he knew I had cried anyway. There was no sense in hiding what happened.

As I explained, I said, "I know, I know. I promise I didn't want that to happen, especially in *that* room with some of the people who were in there." He replied, "Well, for obvious reasons, I wasn't allowed to be in the room because of a conflict of interest with you as my admin mentee. But man, I wish I could have been in there to direct the questions in a different way."

I thanked him for listening, and he said, "Ya know? I can't say I know what's going to happen from here, but I can say I'll do my best to continue to advocate for you. I've seen what you have done here, and I know you would make an excellent assistant principal." I told him I appreciated him for that and turned to leave.

Three very long weeks went by after the interview as we inched towards the end of the summer break. It was long enough for me to start setting up my classroom to teach the following school year, and I almost conceded in my mind that my own assessment was accurate—I would not be getting that job. So, I moved forward and did what I had to do, despite very much wanting to have a new experience in my career and start the next school year in a new role.

Then, very unexpectedly, just three days before the first day of school for every high school in the district, I got a phone call. The phone call came from one of the assistant superintendents who was in my interview three weeks prior. He did not participate in the line of questioning during the interview, but was rather an active listener and observer. He was also my former elementary school principal.

He said, "Amy, we have a spot for you."
I was placed at a different school in the district that I had never been to, and people rarely hear of because of where it is located in the city.

He continued, "I know you can do it. Just get in there and show them you can." So, in seventy-two hours, I packed up my classroom, said my goodbyes to all of my teacher friends from the last seven years, and reorganized to prepare for my first day as an assistant principal.

In the three years that I was in that role at that particular school—you know, the school that they questioned whether or not I had the ability to lead— we graduated more students in the three years that I was leading the high school than in the previous ten years combined. There was a documentary made about the work that our administration, community, and staff had done to wrap comprehensive services around the entire student body and their families, and it was one of the most rewarding experiences I've had in my career. I also made sure that I never cried in front of another peer over a personal matter ever again, because apparently that was not a safe thing to do in this district and then it just became habit.

I tell this story because it is a perfect example of what divides us and the central idea of this book: the imbalance between empathy and power. My experience in the interrogation room was only a small example of a larger, systemic issue at hand in our country. I can tell you that my principal mentor in this story exemplified empathy. The interviewer who checked on me during the five-minute break in my interview exemplified empathy. As we know from the world-renowned voice on empathy, Brené Brown, empathy is *not* sympathy. Brown says, "Empathy is feeling *with* people."[1] In those moments, those two people felt my emotional response about my dad and the intense pressure of the interview, and comforted me. They imagined what it was like to be in my shoes during the interview, how I grieved my dad still, and offered support accordingly. They didn't scold me, and they didn't simply write me off as unqualified or incapable. They saw *me* and gave me the moment I needed to process the event.

In contrast, the people who executed a power dynamic in that interview used that power to manipulate and diminish my experience. They dripped with judgment. Their lack of empathy made me feel more stressed and brought out emotions that didn't showcase the depth of who I was as a leader. I froze instead of feeling free to show what I could do. There was a clear imbalance of empathy and power in the interviewer, who used their position of authority in the room to make me feel small and attempt to prevent my career advancement. It was a microcosm of what is happening in America and across the world.

In my work as a leader in developing, shifting, and improving workplace culture, I will introduce strategies that have proven to be effective in whole-scale change of entire businesses and in individuals to solve for this imbalance. In the chapters that follow you will see examples of this work and receive thorough instructions on how to complete exercises for yourself before working with others, if your goal is to also do this work in teams.

⚠ Activity Alert!

Throughout the book, you will see this symbol: which will indicate an activity or exercise for you/your team to complete. Most of the activities are self-reflective, but some may require you to have conversations with others around you to help you identify blind spots in how you interact with empathy and power in your own life and relationships. Some exercises may vary in how you complete them, depending on whether you are working through this content individually or with a team/organization.

Now is a good time for you to pause and grab your favorite journal or notebook (or a new one), and a pen and/or highlighter. I am old-school and love the feel of writing versus typing. Of course, there are a lot of tech options as well, so feel free to use your tablet, laptop, phone, or any other electronic device where you can journal or jot down thoughts. Keep in mind that these activities will be something you may want to return to on several occasions while reading the book, as well as in the future, as you continue your personal work with empathy and power, or when working with a team and in need of some material resources to use as examples in the team's learning process.

Going Through This Book as an Individual vs. With a Team

In the solution framework in the latter chapters of the book, you will find that there are more targeted activities for leaders and teams. This is intentional. The majority of decisions that impact America's systems and organizations are made by those in positions of power—whether it's within corporate organizations, non-profits, or those in higher positions of government. Many of these leaders are responsible for setting laws and holding power when making sweeping decisions that can change the livelihood of all Americans. All leaders play a pivotal role in American culture and can either perpetuate division by abusing their power and creating an either/or thinking mindset, *or* can influence the healing of division by correcting the imbalance between empathy and power as a role model for balanced leadership.

While the solution is geared towards those in leadership, any of the steps of the solution can be framed for individuals, those who are on small teams or in any organization, and want to make a difference. I must make this clear: this book is designed to heal America, and the only direct way to do that is by starting with individuals and teams who can help to change what leadership looks like. More specifically, I focus on correcting imbalances in leaders who assume positions of power in organizations that have a substantial financial or legislative impact on how our country is run and operated. Those who may get the most out of this book are people in positions of influence within various businesses and organizations or schools across the United States who feel senior leaders are either abusing power or not utilizing their power enough.

It can also greatly benefit independent teams within a business that want to work better, more efficiently, and make more sound decisions together.

There are an infinite number of variables, nuances, and factors involved in working with humans and human relationships. As you work through and confront challenging human behaviors, you may encounter resistance and different emotional responses within yourself and others. The framework, activities, and exercises do not give you a specific template for what to say or do in every situation that you may encounter. What it *does provide are ways to navigate difficult conversations or situations with empathy and, in some cases, the proper amount of power*. I have heard people say, "I'm afraid of saying the wrong thing, so just tell me what to say," and that just isn't possible. No one person can be around for every single event that occurs to tell the other the exact words to say in every situation. If that is what you are searching for, this book will not do that for you. It will, however, provide perspective to understand how to lead yourself and others towards a balance of empathy and power.

To begin our discussion, in Chapter Two, I dive into exactly what empathy is (and isn't) and how to recognize it in our day-to-day lives. When I have led workshops about emotional intelligence, I often ask people in the workshop to define empathy, and I often get responses like "walking in someone else's shoes," "listening," or "removing judgment," and all of those are great ways to generalize empathy. The upcoming chapter dives deeper into the multiple definitions of empathy and details how to learn and develop empathy. It is not a fixed trait one is born with, but a learned skill. You will learn more as you read on.

CHAPTER 2:
No. Like Really!
But What Is Empathy?

The word empathy is often overused and rarely fully understood. It seems like an easy-to-understand concept, but it is often misinterpreted these days, and at times, used as a buzzword and sign of weakness or synonymous with a negative trait. Unfortunately, the term is also becoming a bit politicized and tossed around to characterize particular mindsets or political beliefs.

Susan Lanzoni, author of *Empathy: A History*, wrote a piece about the origin of empathy for Yale University Press. According to her research, "The English term for empathy was coined in 1908 because English-speaking psychologists needed translations of the German scientific terms appearing in the new discipline of experimental psychology."[2] It originates from the German word *Einfühlung*, which means "in-feeling." She goes on to say that after several decades, psychologists extended empathy to the understanding of other people—as a way to truly understand someone else's emotions—which led to the introduction of interpersonal empathy as a study in the social sciences, or what we now call sociology.

Empathy is often mistaken for sympathy or pity, or some other emotion that is not in fact empathy. There are a lot of people in this world who think they know what empathy is, and while Brené Brown, the empathy G.O.A.T., has a hotel on Empathy Boardwalk on the Empathy monopoly board, I'll do my best to take a closer look at, demystify, and clarify empathy.

Merriam-Webster Dictionary defines empathy in the following ways:

1. The action of *understanding*, being *aware of*, being *sensitive* to, and *vicariously* experiencing the *feelings, thoughts*, and experiences of another.

2. The act of *imagining* one's ideas, *feelings*, or *attitudes* as *fully inhabiting* something observed (such as a work of art or natural occurrence).[3]

Let the italicized words sink in for meaning. That singular word, empathy, has quite a bit of meaning inside of it and requires action, which may take time to develop and strengthen. Similar to the word love, empathy is a word that may be used often, and the meaning of it is assumed. The word "love" is an action word. It's complex, just like empathy, and the way that people receive and give love is different for everyone, but that does not mean we stop trying to do it or feel it.

Once more, go back and read the definitions and pause over the italicized words. As you pause on those words, think about what it takes to develop each one in oneself, let alone all of them together at once, and to exemplify them for others. Continue to let that rest in your mind as you read about the following example of empathy.

Empathy in Action

I have found in my teaching experience that when something is misinterpreted or defined improperly, it is helpful to describe the concept or term using an example, scenario, or story.

To apply this method to understanding empathy, I want to refer to a scenario from Brené Brown who as I introduced earlier, describes empathy as "feeling with people," or finding a way to connect someone else's journey to an experience of your own.[4] She goes on to clarify that rarely does being empathetic start with the phrase, "at least." You don't *compare* someone else's experience to your own. You use your experience to connect with others so that *they* (not you) feel seen, heard, and valued. For example, if someone close to you shares that their father has recently passed away, a response like, "Well, at least you still have your mother," is not empathy. An empathetic response might sound like, "Wow. I can imagine how you're feeling after experiencing the loss of my own father. I'm here for you if you ever need an ear." Maybe, in the weeks following, you drop off a meal for your friend, because you know how hard it was for you to muster the energy to cook when you were in the depths of your grief when you lost your father.

If people live long enough lives and face adversity, at some point or another, they will probably encounter people who attempt empathy and yet deliver sympathy. Sympathy is a surface-level response, avoiding the personal feelings required to understand someone else. It is a hands-off and non-feeling response. Sympathy is not a bad emotion to feel or action towards another that results in harm, but it can sometimes feel like the bare minimum. Sympathy can be defined as having concern for or pity for someone who may be experiencing something difficult or painful.

To further illustrate what sympathy is and how it is different from empathy, I'll give an example from one of my guilty TV pleasures, *Queen Charlotte: A Bridgerton Story* (Netflix). Shonda Rhimes, the show's creator, is an absolute genius. In one episode of the show, the queen's personality is far from showing empathy to almost everyone she encounters, and if she does have empathy, she conceals it through a gift or a minimal kind gesture. She more often represents the stoic, cold, pompous, colonial portrayal of royalty. Towards the middle of the season's episodes, her son—Prince George—loses his daughter. The writers turn a very tragic situation into something comical in this scene:

Prince George was inconsolable and uncontrollably sobbing over the loss of his daughter and unborn grandchild, sitting bent over at the waist with his head in his hands in a fancy green velvet chair. He wore a full colonial-style suit, complete with a white ruffled shirt. His head was buried while his body shook as he wept. The satire and over-the-top dramatics are so much so that you can't help but chuckle.

Queen Charlotte arrived in her enormous dress—the kind with the under skirt that makes the dress appear to have built-in shelving on both sides of the gown—and her very big, ornate colonial hair. She walked to the back of his chair and was just close enough to him to reach his back with a pat of her hand, which you can tell she was uninterested in doing. Her body language and facial expression also made it clear she didn't want to deal with any of this. Then, with a low and driest tone imaginable and a strong British accent, she proclaimed, "Sorrows, sorrows... prayers." Her voice bordered on annoyance. Yet, she did indeed express her *sympathy*, which, gentle readers, is not empathy. (And if you watch the show, you know what I just did there).[5]

If Queen Charlotte acted with empathy, she would have sat with her son and comforted him. She may have looked him in the eyes (not stood behind him and barely interacted), and said things like, "I can't understand how you are feeling, but I'm here with you supporting you," or "I know this is a difficult thing to comprehend, I remember when I went through it myself. How can I best support you at this tough time?" She may have sat and *imagined* her son's pain, felt a glimpse of it herself, and even shared a small part of her own story so that her son did not feel alone in that moment. Even her non-verbal body language could have expressed genuine concern and interest in wanting to be present as a support for her son.

When we learn how to demonstrate empathy, the impact is as much for us as it is for the person to whom we show empathy. We can be positively changed by experiencing empathy—becoming aware of what others are going through, imagining their experience vividly, and feeling it as if we were experiencing their situation ourselves. When we do this, especially for those experiencing the symptoms of the imbalance of empathy and power, we understand a situation better without experiencing it firsthand, and we become more motivated to do something about an unjust situation.

Activity: Empathy Definition Reflection

Grab your journaling resources (whether paper, pen, or technology-based) and reflect on each of the italicized words in the definitions above, and journal about the following:

Key Empathy Definition Terms:

Understanding, aware of, sensitive to, vicariously, feelings, thoughts, imagining, fully inhabiting

Reflection Questions:

✦ What comes to mind when you think about what each of the italicized words means to you? For example, when I see the word "understanding," I think about interactions I may have had with my kids when I had to be more understanding when they didn't know how to do something. Write down a few word associations or memories associated with the terms above.

✦ Journal about separate occasions when you actively showed *understanding, awareness*, or *sensitivity* to another person, or received it or experienced it for yourself.

✦ Next, journal about a time when you *vicariously* lived through someone else's feelings and thoughts. For example, when one of my friends goes to a vacation destination that I have never been to but want to go to, I try to imagine what they are thinking and feeling during their travels. I would write about what I was thinking and feeling, and what it was like living that experience through their thoughts and feelings.

✦ Next, journal about a time that you had to imagine others' ideas, feelings, and attitudes about a particular subject or person. For example, I could journal about what I imagine one of my favorite musical artists was thinking about while writing song lyrics and how their feelings or attitude created the idea for the song.

✦ Finally, use this statement as a prompt: "The last time I showed empathy for someone else was..." and explain when you showed empathy for someone using the definitions of the word above. For example, you might start with, "The last time I showed empathy for someone else was when I showed understanding for . . ." Then, answer the following questions:

> o What was the outcome of that experience?
>
> o What impact did it have on you and on the person (or people) with whom the experience included?

Now that you know what empathy is and how it differs from sympathy, thanks to our friends Brené Brown and Queen Charlotte, and your own personal work investigating the meaning of the word, I want to dig a bit deeper into how empathy shows up differently in various stages of life, as well as in our personal or professional relationships.

How Empathy Develops in Humans

In order to learn how to grow empathy as an adult, it is important to know how empathy develops throughout your lifetime. The development of empathy is influenced by various factors. If you are going to play a role in helping others develop their empathy, having this knowledge will provide foundational information you can use to teach them. Some people may need to go back to early developmental uses of empathy in order to move towards a more mature understanding of what empathy is and how to show it towards other adults.

Because empathy is such a complex concept to develop and master, it manifests differently at various stages of human development. According to neuroscientific research published in "The Neurodevelopment of Empathy in Humans," empathy engages specific parts of the brain at different stages of development.[6] Some development of empathy involving emotional understanding happens as early as the age of two to three years old, and positive social behaviors as a reaction to comforting someone else can develop as early as twelve to eighteen months old. However, more mature abilities, like the ability to take the perspective of another, do not start to develop until around six to eleven years old. This continues into the teen years when, eventually, the ability to control emotions, engage with emotional regulation, and inhibit negative emotions begins around or after the age of sixteen.

Interestingly, as people age into adulthood, research shows that there is a gradual change in the brain's response from a visceral to a more evaluative function. In other words, empathy at younger ages is felt more deeply in the body, while in older adults, empathy is used in the more judgmental and discerning parts of the brain. I highly encourage you to explore Appendix A (pg. 18) and read through how these younger stages develop. It will help you learn how to best approach adults or discern whether someone's early developmental experiences have affected them. Below, I expand more on how empathy shows up in adults and in the workplace.

Adults

Becoming an adult is a long process. Sometimes I feel like I am still figuring it out. Needless to say, there are a gazillion (yes, gazillion) different life experiences that can exemplify how we show and receive empathy in our adult lives. In college, you may have shown empathy to a friend who was sad because their boyfriend or girlfriend went to a school in a different city or town that was further than regular travel would allow. You may have learned how to show empathy when a coworker at your first job shared that they were let go because of staffing cuts. You may have had to be empathetic when one of your friends was the only one in the friend group who had not found a lifetime partner or gotten married yet. You may have practiced empathy with your own children, witnessing them experience life for the first time. You may have extended empathy when a close friend lost a loved one unexpectedly. All of these examples are just a tiny glimpse into the numerous ways and how often empathy can be shown.

The storied example I have from my adult life of showing empathy is a hard one to share. I lost my dad to kidney disease when I was twenty-seven years old. My dad lived a full life and was a much older dad than most people my age might have had. But nonetheless, he was gone before he even got to meet his first grandson. My mom lived almost sixteen years without him, but was diagnosed with mild cognitive impairment just two years after he passed away. It was a long road and journey with her as her condition developed into Alzheimer's disease, and she passed away in 2022. It is hard going through the period of life when you are now the caretaker of your parents, especially at a time when you still need their guidance. Not having living parents to lean on and ask questions to, while still raising your own kids, is very difficult. And yet, it has also given me earlier insight into what it means to be a caregiver of adults and children simultaneously. It has allowed me to help others who are in situations like this, no matter how old they are.

Most recently, one of my close personal friends lost her mother after a long fight with multiple myeloma. Her mother was also my dear sorority sister. As I was assisting my friend with funeral plans and helping to guide her through the process, the absolute best that I could, there were several times that I found myself getting caught up in my own continued process of grief for my own mother. Just like my friend, my mom was one of my best friends on this planet, and losing her to Alzheimer's was a slow torture. On top of it all, learning how to live with the realization that I am a "matriarch" on our side of the family was daunting and still is to this day. Yet, I still had to be there for my friend.

In my sorority, there is a special public ceremony that can occur for the deceased sorority sister at her or the family's request. My friend's mother requested this ceremony, and I was asked to step up and deliver the sorority eulogy on behalf of one of my second mothers and my sorority sister. Empathy also involves removing your own desires and stepping into a position to be what a person needs you to be for them in that moment. While extremely difficult, I had to step outside of myself to think of what my friend and her mother would want, and what would help them feel more comfortable at that sensitive moment, not what I would want. I did it. I was visibly shaking through the entire thing to keep from crying, but I did it.

This story is an example of empathy for another when they may or may not even know you have demonstrated it to them. It is not a self-pat on the back, yet it is an example of drawing on something you have experienced yourself that may have been painful or difficult, and using it to connect to someone else who needed you to step up for them in an empathetic way. At times, they may not even know you are doing that. This is empathy with integrity—doing the right thing even when no one is paying attention or is aware.

Learning Empathy at Work

Empathy at work, especially when in positions of leadership, looks very similar to empathy in other environments but has some special nuances. Work relationships are encouraged to be cordial, honest, friendly, dependable, responsible, and trusting, which probably doesn't sound much different than characteristics that make up a good friendship. The difference is that not everyone at work will get along with one another or would "choose" to be friends with one another outside of work.

Creating an effective and trusting work relationship takes effort, whether it is peer-to-peer, manager-to-employee, or executive-to-board of directors. According to a research report from Seramount, a research organization that is a subsidiary of EAB, there are seven components that can be identified in any relationship. They are described as the seven pillars of connectivity. They are:

- ☐ Personal Background
- ☐ Sense of Humor
- ☐ Language/Dialect
- ☐ Political/Social Morals
- ☐ Interests/Hobbies
- ☐ Shared Life Trajectory
- ☐ Musical Preferences[7]

Seramount's research indicates that at least four of these seven criteria must be present for a relationship to be successful (in their context, it was referencing a mentor relationship).

1. Look at the list a little closer and think about someone that you are close to, whether it is your spouse, a close friend, a sibling, or a family member, and see if you can identify four or more of these pillars that you share with that person. You can even check them off if you like, with a small check mark in the small boxes next to each pillar.

2. Now, think of someone in your life who you are not close to or in your past where the relationship (regardless of its nature) did not work well and was not successful.

    a. Did you align with that person on at least four of the pillars above? You can place an X to the right of the pillars above.

3. Were any of those relationships with people you worked with and you had to find a way to make it work anyway? How did you resolve that?

Seramount researchers make it clear that each of the seven pillars is not needed for a successful relationship, which is why you may be very close to people and still not agree on things that may be of significance personally. I can think of several people that I know and love and are close to me, and we do not agree on musical preferences, or have vastly different personal backgrounds, but the other qualities exist between us, and our relationship just works.

However, this is in regard to personal relationships—you know, the ones we have choices to pursue or not. How do we incorporate this into work, where we don't always get to pick who we interact with on our teams? In my work as a corporate executive, I was tasked with creating a mentoring and sponsorship program. A mentoring software company released an article called: "The Importance of Pairings in Mentorship Programs." This article, as well as additional research completed by organizations that create mentoring software programs for businesses, argue that the success of these programs are contingent upon successful matching of mentor to mentee.[8] Using the seven pillars of connectivity to create an assessment for interested mentors and mentees, it was a vital part to ensuring program success. As of the publication of this book, there is a 98% success rate in the matching of mentees to mentors in this program rated by the participants themselves. This demonstrates the accuracy and reliability of the research that those four to seven criteria must align.

So, what does this have to do with empathy at work? Well, not all work relationships have four of these seven pillars shared between them, but you won't know what you have in common with others unless you take the time to assess it. One way you can do this is by having leaders draft a survey that addresses each of those seven pillars and have teams or pairs of people take the survey to determine where they match, and in which pillars they don't, and then have discussions about how to work better together. It can also lead to fun discussions that may have nothing to do with work, but will help to build stronger connections and relationships to enhance trust and empathy.

Yet, sometimes those pillars won't align well, and regardless of that, people at work must find a way to trust each other enough to get their work done, especially if they are on the same teams. Again, remember that it doesn't matter if the communication is peer-to-peer, supervisor/manager-to-direct report, or leader-to-leader. At some point, you may encounter someone who thinks differently from you or does not share your interests, but requires empathy. To be successful in creating a trusting work relationship, we have to channel our empathy. This means imagining what someone else is going through, either at work or at home, what their workload might feel like, or how they could best be supported, even if they aren't asking for it. And to be clear, it is not always the responsibility of the direct report to ask. It should start with the leaders first.

There are other scenarios at work when empathy is needed and while they may be no different than empathy you would show to someone in your personal life, the added layer of being a manager to someone or having a professional relationship and expecting a particular work output, with the responsibility of ensuring the business maintains a level of success and performance, makes it difficult.

Let's look at the following scenario to help illustrate this tricky dynamic to help you navigate what this looks like at work:

A sales executive, Ben, is leading a team of seven sales representatives for a pharmaceutical product. There are two very high performers on the team, Siobhan and David, who Ben counts on to hit their sales quotas each month, quarter, and year. He can depend on them because in the three years that they have been reporting to him on his team, their team has exceeded their sales targets for the business. One week before mid-year reporting, which is a critical time for this team to hit milestones and report to the higher-ups, David reaches out to Ben and discloses that his wife is experiencing pregnancy complications and may have to take family leave for an undetermined amount of time if she is placed on bed rest. Ben knows that if he loses David for one week, let alone five weeks, the chance of the team hitting their sales goals will suffer. To make matters worse, one of the other sales reps just resigned, which leaves Ben's team one person short. How does Ben handle David's situation in an empathetic way, while still plowing towards the sales goals? Ben is stressed out because the performance of his team and missing sales quotas means reduced earnings, fewer bonuses, and perhaps the loss of additional sales incentives.

Of course, there are several ways that Ben could address the issues, but here is one example of a way he can handle things empathetically with David:

Ben is also married and has a two-year-old daughter. He and David are not particularly close outside of work, but they depend on each other at work to reach sales goals. Ben remembers how hard it was for him to return to the demands of work when his daughter was born, and thinks about how difficult it would have been to concentrate on anything if he knew his wife and daughter's lives were at risk. Ben pauses to reflect on this and then calls David. Ben says, "I can't imagine what this must feel like for you, and I want you to know that the team is here for you, however we can be. Please take the time you need. Before you go, can we set up a meeting to chat through some of your deals, and maybe you can give me some suggestions on some other team members you have worked with so we can see those deals through in your absence?"

That is empathy at work. Ben and David might not become best friends—maybe they don't share all or even just four of the pillars of connectivity—but Ben was still able to access empathy and support David. This probably made David feel seen and supported, and might have confirmed that this workplace would continue to fit his life even after having a daughter.

Moments of empathy can impact people's lives in dramatic ways. Sometimes those moments happen in the workplace, and sometimes they happen in our daily lives outside of work. Most of the time, they can create lasting change for the people on the receiving end, as well as the giving. The following activity will allow you to investigate how the presence of empathy or lack of empathy can affect how people engage and get along with others, even those you may not know personally.

Activity: An Exercise In Empathy Using Two Short Stories

As we become adults, we meet people who are different than us. They may come from different places and have backstories we couldn't imagine. Let's examine the topic of empathy further through the following two short stories. Both of the stories are taken from factual events, but in some cases, the names are changed to illustrate a point.

Short Story: The Military Men

Back in the early 1800s, there lived a woman named Adella. She was born into slavery, her father was the plantation owner, and her mother was a slave. She grew up on a plantation in Tennessee but was later sent to Virginia. Luckily, Adella was not separated from her first two children, and they all went together to Virginia. She married a man there, Mr. Skinner, on the slave grounds. For those who may not know, slaves established their union by jumping over a broom. In the absence of a legal right to marry, it represented them sweeping away their old lives and entering a new one together. Everyone on the plantation, even the owners, was aware of this practice.

Unfortunately, after they had a child, Mr. Skinner became abusive towards Adella. She made the decision to flee the plantation and slavery altogether with her children, braving the underground railroad from Virginia to Ohio. For those that aren't aware, the underground railroad was not an actual train. I highly recommend researching what that experience was like for those seeking freedom from slavery. If you are a parent or mother, you may empathize with the fear, courage, and protection she felt along the way while trying to keep her children safe simply to be free. With help, Adella made it over the Ohio River and decided to settle there as a newly "free" woman.

After getting settled, Adella met a man named Samuel, and he was very kind. They later married and had two more daughters, Sarah and Corintha. Sarah grew up just before the Emancipation Proclamation was signed, and all slaves were freed by 1865. At some point, Adella and Samuel split, and she later met a man named George, and they had six children together: four boys and two girls. In total, Adella now had eleven children.

One of their children, Arthur, grew up in Cincinnati and was drafted into the Army during WWI. He was deployed and shipped off to France to serve and protect the country that enslaved his mother and his descendants. He felt a strong desire to see the world and serve others, and was proud to be a part of the military. After his service, he returned home and was fortunate enough to find a fantastic job for a Black man in the early 1900s as a U.S. Postal Service employee. It was then that he met a woman named Sally Williams.

Sally was special to Arthur. She was very fair-skinned, and for a while before meeting Arthur, she had cut her hair very short and was "passing" as White. Her father was a white man, although he did not claim her as his own, she did receive some early education and privileges as a result. You may wonder why Sally would choose to "pass". Passing was a common practice in those times for fair-skinned black women who might pass as White to survive the racial climate, pursue an education or career interest and perhaps access privileges that were only available for White people at that time. Sally was taught how to play classical piano in her childhood and had become so good at it that she was offered to play in concert halls across the city. That opportunity only existed because she passed for a White woman to get into some of those venues. It didn't take long after meeting and falling in love with Arthur that she realized she couldn't and did not want to live the difficult and sometimes dangerous life of trying to pass as a White woman anymore. For many women that experienced "passing" in those times, eventually it feels like a lie or like you are denying part of your own heritage. She decided to live an authentic life as a Black woman but kept the 1897 baby grand piano gifted to her and went to school to be certified as a preschool teacher.

Sally got a teaching position at one of the segregated schools for Black children in Cincinnati, and Arthur and Sally's love story unfolded as they married and had two children, Arthur Jr. and Betty. They were a middle-class black family in the early 1900s, which was very rare at that time. They lived a happy life, in a nice home in a safe Black neighborhood. They regularly attended the neighborhood Episcopalian church with their friends and neighbors alike. Betty was very smart and went on to attend a high school that has become a historical building in the Cincinnati area, and one with a phenomenal academic legacy across the United States. She attended the school because her aunt, who was one of the first few Black female graduates of that school, encouraged her to do so. Betty then went to the local university, where she studied French with the goal of moving overseas to be a French interpreter for the war after graduation. Her brother, Arthur Jr., was quite the athlete, but Arthur Jr. chose a different high school than Betty because he didn't want to live in her shadows as the "smart girl's little brother." As a result, Arthur Jr. ended up having a very different experience.

You see, while Arthur Jr. was visibly Black, his skin tone was on the lighter side as well—more of a bronze tone that some may associate with the color of a copper penny in the summer, when his melanin was at its strongest, but in the winter it faded to a light creamed coffee tone. He had a very deep voice as a teenager, very similar to the legendary actor and orator, James Earl Jones, who most people know as the voice of Darth Vader from the *Star Wars* films and Mufasa from the animated Disney feature, *The Lion King*. Arthur Jr. really wanted to sing in the choir to please his mom, Sallie, who taught her daughter on the baby grand Baldwin piano and continued to play herself at home.

When Arthur Jr. showed interest in the school choir, the choir teacher responded, "Yes, Arthur, you can be in the choir, but in order to do so, you have to perform in the minstrel shows we have." Arthur Jr., who wanted so badly to be in the choir, complied. If you have never seen or heard of the minstrel shows in the early 1900s, they are hard to watch now. Minstrel shows were the birth of blackface, and White actors would put black shoe polish on their faces, and exaggerated red or white lips to distort an image of the facial features of African Americans.[9] These shows were a poor attempt at comedy, with music and plot lines of Black culture driving the performance. Arthur Jr. was asked to wear blackface in the minstrel show as a teenager because he was told he wasn't dark enough to be Black. Again, with no other choice to make, Arthur Jr. complied, and to his satisfaction, he was one of the only Black members of the school choir. Once in the choir, he faced continued hardships as he was given no music, and when they performed, he was required to look down at his hands rather than up at the director.

After graduating from high school as a football standout, he was offered the chance to play football as a tight end at Howard University in Washington, D.C. He was tall and had a great football build, and was soon being recruited to play football at West Point. At that time, he would have been the first Black man to play football there (as he told it), but unfortunately, Arthur Jr. was drafted into the Army during the latter part of WWII and was deployed to Japan just as he was about to accept the football scholarship to play for their defense. In the Army, he was only nineteen years old and quickly rose through the ranks, becoming one of the youngest (if not the youngest) Black drill sergeants at that time. Sadly, he was honorably discharged when his sister Betty tragically and suddenly passed away during an operation to remove a hernia. He returned home to Ohio to care for his family.

Despite all of the hardships that he faced in his early life, Arthur Jr. decided that he would change the face of the business community in Cincinnati. He went on to get two college degrees in Business and Business Administration and was the first Black man to serve on several boards, civic organizations, and positions in the business community. He lived a full life, having had two wives, four children, and a successful career. There were several headlines in newspapers about their family and about Arthur Jr. when he passed, one that read, "Prominent Black family loses a legend." Arthur Jr. is even written about in local historical books for his accomplishments. There were several people along this journey who balanced empathy with power to help guide Arthur, Jr., towards a successful life despite the obstacles he faced.

Short Story #2: The Gentle Giant Athlete

There lived a man named Paul. He was born into slavery in North Carolina, and after the Civil War, he was able to gain his freedom. Paul was a very smart man. He was savvy and knew how to work a crowd. He knew that to gain wealth and maintain his freedom, he needed to buy land. He found a way to do so and quickly amassed a great amount of wealth in land ownership. He worked this land with his own hands alongside his growing family. He was a tall man with a commanding stature, and many of his male children held these same physical traits.

By the early 1900s, Paul met a man who convinced him to sell his property so that he had tangible cash. In the process of that sale, there were some fraudulent tax transactions and bad business deals that prevented Paul from transferring any of his land or its cash holdings to his descendants upon his death. It is believed that someone took advantage of him and his lack of tax education, and as a result, his family was left with nothing. They were forced to sell off the land and lose the investment in their hard work in order to get the money just to survive. His family was left to figure it all out, starting over, and for generations, they struggled to get ahead in a community that was unwilling to give them a chance.

Many generations later, one of Paul's great-great-grandchildren, Allen, grew up to be a very tall, slender man. Allen was born in North Carolina, like his ancestors, but his family moved to Texas. In high school in the 1980s, his family had little to nothing financially, in a community that had little to nothing to offer. Allen wasn't the best at the academic part of school. Like some teen boys, he wasn't very interested in the academic parts of school and didn't receive the help he may have needed to succeed academically. It was then that people in the school and his surrounding family convinced Allen that the best way to get bigger and have a good chance at a better life was through sports. He started playing football and basketball, and soon his body filled out and he was a stud of an athlete. He became co-captain of the basketball team as a power forward and a tight end on the football team. Ironically, the same football position just like Arthur Jr. in the previous story. Sure enough, it landed Allen the opportunity to play football in college.

Allen was the life of the party and had a big personality. Everyone knew him or wanted to know him, and he had a knack for making everyone feel safe around him. He was a big guy, and some were intimidated by his stature as he grew to six foot six, but Allen was the guy everyone loved to be around. He would reassure people all the time that he wasn't going to hurt them because he could sense people feeling threatened by his stature, and he just wanted to have fun and be a part of the group. While he was in college, he played in a Texas State championship, and later transferred to a school in South Florida. Being away was tougher on him than he thought it would be. Allen felt like he couldn't find his place there and didn't have the support of his family nearby. Like many students who get homesick, he decided to return home to Texas.

Once back home, he got a job customizing cars and still played basketball. He didn't want his tall frame to get thin again so he maintained exercise. One night, while walking home from a game, he had just gotten across the street from his house, and he was stopped by a police officer who asked him where he was going. He replied with a smile, "I'm just about to head into my house right there, Officer. Would you like to see my license with my address on it?" The police officer told him not to move, and he arrested him for trespassing in his own neighborhood. Allen was puzzled and saddened by this because he didn't do anything wrong. Over time, the profiling and racism got worse. It felt like Allen was being targeted for some reason, and the police in that area kept antagonizing him. Soon, he started to feel like he had made a bad decision coming back home and was beating himself up over those mistakes. Through his sadness, lack of support, and inability to move forward, he felt paralyzed. Like many who struggle with mental health burdens, he tried to numb his mistakes and pain with opioids and alcohol. He soon became addicted to them and started making even poorer decisions. Allen began to rob and steal to fund his habits, like many who become addicted to substances do.

Addiction is a relentless and difficult disease because it eats away at a person's ability to trust their own judgment or break free from the cycle it causes. It would be easier to understand how addiction works and affects the brain simply by thinking about coffee. Many corporate executives can't make it through the day without reloading their coffee cups. They start the day with caffeine, and when it fades, their brains tell them it's time for more. If they don't fill up, they get headaches, nausea, jitters, and more. As it turns out, though, coffee is legal even though it has lasting, detrimental physical effects on the body. The same applies to those with a dependency on stimulants other than caffeine.

Allen later graduated from opioids to a more serious drug habit and was arrested for theft with a deadly weapon when he raided someone's apartment looking for money. He never knew that someone was in the apartment and would never hurt anyone, but Allen was not himself. He was sentenced to prison for five years but was released within four. When Allen was released, he was sober, and he wanted to make better decisions. He knew in order to live a different life, he had to leave Texas, and he had to get help for his addiction. He found a specialized rehabilitation program in Minnesota, and he moved there immediately. He found a good job and even shared a great townhome with a roommate that he met in his rehab program. Things were looking up for Allen, and he was feeling really good about the turn of direction for his life.

One day, he left for work, had a great day, and returned to his townhome in a great middle-class neighborhood. He felt like he was finally living the life he was meant to live and was proud of himself. He got home and found his roommate lying on the couch. He went over to wake him, but he didn't wake up. His roommate had unfortunately overdosed, and he passed away. Allen was shocked and devastated all over again. This was the first time he allowed someone into his personal world and trusted them after everything that happened. It seemed like his friend was all in with him on the road to recovery. He was distraught, and all of the bad thoughts about failure started to creep in again. He decided to take a walk to a nearby gas station for some air and juice, and he ran into an old friend who asked how he was doing. Allen broke down. He told his friend that he was in a very dark place again, and unfortunately, it didn't take long for Allen to relapse.

Over time, Allen went through several periods of getting sober and relapsing back into drugs again. He was arrested a couple of times because of drug addiction. He held several jobs that seemed to be going well, but when he had to take morning classes to keep one of the jobs, he was forced to drop out because it conflicted with his ability to earn money for his family. He did have romantic relationships and had five children, all of whom he felt the responsibility to support, but Allen was never able to shake the losses and his own trauma. He was later hospitalized for an accidental overdose but recovered and was released.

Not long after, he went to the corner store that he frequented. His six-foot-six frame had shrunk over time with continued drug use and the hard parts of his life, but he was still a tall six-foot-four. He went to pay for his item, and the clerk thought he was using a counterfeit bill. Accordingly, the clerk called the police, unbeknownst to Allen. He was sitting in his car with a friend when the police arrived. They pulled him from the car, put him on the ground face down, and restrained him with handcuffs. The police officer who restrained him was using extreme force to hold him there, and soon, people who were watching on the street became concerned for Allen because he stopped moving and talking. Allen was carried away on a stretcher to the hospital, where he was confirmed dead. Allen's headlines read very differently from Arthur Jr.'s headlines.

If you are familiar with the events of 2020 in America, you may have now figured out that Allen is George Floyd.[10] You do not know that the first story was about my family and my father, Arthur, Jr. While the stories are very different, both men faced adversity and hardships based on what they looked like and who they were in society at that time. They both had to make accommodations for others to feel accepted or fit into the areas they wanted to be and the people they were interested in becoming.

It's time for you to pull out your journal that you started.

Reflect on what the differences are between the two men's stories. Here are questions and prompts to consider:

+ What did one man have that the other man did not have?
+ At what point could empathy from others have changed the course of either man's life?
+ Was one family shown more empathy at some point than another? How so and by whom?
+ At what point in each story did you begin to have thoughts and feelings about Arthur Jr.? About Allen?
+ Were those thoughts and feelings rooted in concern and care? Or did you find yourself feeling contempt or judgment?
+ If you had encountered Allen or Arthur at various difficult stages of their journey, how could you have responded to either Allen or Arthur in a way that might have made a difference in their journey? Be specific about a time in their lives as an example.

After you have examined your thoughts and answers to the questions above, think about how you view the actions of others that you do not know. Write some thoughts and responses to the following questions:

+ Did you see a story in the media or anywhere in mainstream news that gave the full story of George Floyd's life?
+ How do you think the way we are told about others influences how we respond to them empathetically (or not)?
+ Do you take the time to truly learn about a person and their background prior to making judgments/showing empathy (or not)?
+ Ask others if they have heard you say or act in response to various events involving people that you do not know. What kinds of responses do you receive? What types of things do you say and do from the perspective of others?

Synthesize your responses to these questions and think about how you can improve or hep others around you learn and improve.

Empathy and Unconscious Bias

Humans develop preferences for all things based on their life experiences. This could be as simple as living in different geographic locations and growing up eating pizza instead of sushi, for example. It could also be related to who you grew up around as well. These preferences get categorized in our minds and trick us into thinking that what we do is what all people do. Maybe the people around us growing up made us think that all people look the same, sound alike, live similar lifestyles or many more possibilities, simply because that is our brain's way of putting things into files for easy understanding.

This is called unconscious bias, and it has an effect on how we relate to people and the level of empathy we are able to show towards others that we may or may not know. Unconscious biases develop without people realizing it, and are usually not deliberate or intended to cause harm, but it does cause harm. Harvard University reported that unconscious biases are "snap judgments we make about people and situations based upon years of subconscious socialization."[11] That is a fancy way of restating how I explained it above: our brains, without our conscious permission, categorize information into patterns to lighten our mental load, and that includes categorizing people. It could be as simple as the example below.

When I was a teenager, I was a lifeguard, and there were a lot of moms who brought their kids to the pool every day. Often, there were moms who would reveal their new belly bumps in their bathing suits, and when we got to know the families, we would often comment or wish congratulations on their expanding families. One day, I saw a woman with a bump, whom I had known for several years as a member of the pool I was a lifeguard for, and I went up to her and said, "Congratulations, Mrs. Oliver! I didn't know you were expecting!" And the shock on her face was immediate. She laughed a little, but I could tell it was not a pleasant laugh. And she said, "I'm not pregnant, but now I know I need to hit the gym." I was mortified! I was only sixteen, and my brain put all women with a belly bump into one category without my permission. I would never offend someone on purpose. You can tell how much that affected me because it is now three decades later, and it was like it happened yesterday. My stomach is still in knots about it. I apologized for the entire rest of the day and for the weeks that followed. It was awful, and from that point on, I never commented on another woman's pregnancy unless they announced it first. My lived experiences cause me to unconsciously judge her appearance, and I unknowingly made an assumption about what that meant and unintentionally offended her. That is unconscious bias.

It is important to know that having unconscious bias is not anyone's fault. It develops without us knowing, and *we all have some form of it*. However, we must acknowledge that unconscious bias exists, and when we become aware of something that we may be biased about, it is our responsibility to do our best to learn why and how to operate better or differently. And, if in our own lack of knowing we do cause harm, we must be courageous enough to apologize for it and learn why it caused harm. When we do, the result is an improved sense of empathy for others, sometimes even people we don't know.

It is also important to know that there are people who are overtly biased, prejudiced, or openly demonstrate their hate or disdain for individuals and groups of people. This is a result of being isolated from others and educated in a separatist way that reinforces power control or feeds into the fear of a loss of power if others have equal access. All of these matters are discussed in the next chapter as you investigate all of the aspects of power.

The Pinnacle of Empathy

You may be wondering why reading the short stories and reflecting on them was important to this book. The ultimate pinnacle of empathy is the ability to show it towards someone you may have never met. It is difficult to imagine how a person can show empathy for a stranger. It is a bit easier to have a deeper understanding and awareness of someone you are close to because your relationship is personal. The person means more to you, you might feel their pain more closely, and it is possible for you to see the direct, immediate impact of your empathy on the person who is going through a potentially difficult time. When you hear of someone facing a hardship who you see on TV, or walk by in a grocery store, or hear about in the news, or barely interact with at work, or maybe even dislike, it is harder to connect with them—unless perhaps you are able to hear their story, and it is similar to your own experiences.

But what if their story isn't similar to yours? What if you've never experienced what they've gone through? Do you turn a blind eye and move on with your day?

In these situations, I encourage you to listen and try to understand, and to do that, you may have to learn or create opportunities to observe, read, or even experience the lives of others. Part of what perpetuates the divide among our communities and creates the imbalance of empathy and power is the unwillingness to learn about others and to remove judgment prior to taking action.

Don't get me wrong, this takes intentional effort, but in some cases, it also may not take an extensive amount of time. Terri Givens, author of *Radical Empathy*, discusses how practicing empathy using her six steps can help to heal racial divides. She specifically focuses on the process of understanding thoughts and feelings about your own identity, and then suggests that to heal racial divides that have affected the Black community in particular, it is important to "move beyond an understanding of other's lives and pain to understand the origins of our own biases"—these biases are what have directly affected the Black community.[12] While her book is focused more on one specific population, her points are grounded in the heart of what empathy is: *the willingness to be vulnerable and be open to the experiences of others so that others feel for and want to support those whom they may not even know.*

Empathy is about asking questions to learn how you might connect with someone else, even if you are different from them or do not know them at all. With more empathy comes more connection. More human connection with others brings understanding and the ability to have a more unified existence, instead of a divisive one. Remember that the goal is not to be perfect, yet to try your best to learn.

Ashley Abramson wrote that "in a society marked by increasing division, we could all be a bit more kind, cooperative, and tolerant towards others. Beneficial as those traits are, psychological research suggests empathy may be the umbrella trait required to develop these virtues."[13] The author also quotes Stanford University psychologist Jamil Zaki, PhD, who describes empathy as the "psychological superglue that connects people and undergirds cooperation and kindness"—even if empathy doesn't come naturally, research suggests that it can be cultivated and hopefully improve society as a result.

Further, Andrew R. Todd et al. found that empathy can promote better attitudes towards strangers and be a crucial ingredient in reducing bias and racism.[14] When teachers are trained to build positive relationships with students and value various perspectives, their increased empathy reduces punitive disciplinary consequences.

But what about work? Why does empathy matter at work? Jakob Franzen describes seven benefits that are realized when leaders lean into the skill of building empathy from a leader in their coaching council:

+ Improved communication
+ Increased employee engagement
+ Better problem-solving
+ Enhanced team cohesion
+ Greater adaptability
+ Enhanced reputation
+ Stronger relationships[15]

The evidence is clear: improving empathy has a beneficial outcome for society and the workplace. Empathy (or lack thereof) in the two short stories also demonstrates its intersection with mental health, self-care, and power structures, further indicating the delicate balance that is necessary to maintain between empathy and power. We will examine these intersections in the chapters that follow.

WIIFM – Cue the Eye Roll

As we continue to analyze empathy and power, it might be natural for you to wonder: where do I fit into all of this? When I have spoken about empathy at length in conferences or webinars and the subject matter focuses on putting ourselves in others' shoes, there is usually someone who will bravely ask: But what about me? Where do I fit into all of this?

I have also heard this question come up in my professional life, whether as an educational administrator or as an executive leader. Usually, it arises when I have created a proposal for a project, am seeking approval for a strategy or an initiative from senior leaders, or am circulating an asset for use by an entire staff or department. Often, I am asked if I have considered what others will think when they see it and ask, "What's in it for me?" (Or "WIIFM"). Throughout my career, I have heard so many people ask, "What's the WIIFM on this?"

By nature, my empathy/power balance tips to the empathy side. Anyone close to me will confirm that I typically consider others before myself (most of the time), and therefore, when I am sharing the product of my work for any reason (including this book), I am constantly thinking of others. Admittedly, when I hear the WIIFM question, my initial reaction is a hard eye roll followed by the internal thought, "Do people always need to receive something for themselves? The point is that this isn't about you!" Those thoughts don't last long because my next thought is that I do need to consider what is "in it" for me and for those implementing the work. Also, I need to consider who those people are and what motivates them, just like I did when I wrote this book.

There is nothing wrong with considering what you are going to receive and whether or not it is of value, regardless of the situation, especially if you're being asked to spend your time, energy, and money investing in something. In fact, many would not consider spending their time on something that wouldn't be of measurable value to them. For this reason, there is value in focusing also on reciprocity. To have empathy does not mean that you constantly give empathy away to others without engaging in a healthy two-way relationship, whether that is at work or with a friend. Let's look at this more.

Reciprocity

The idea that someone will receive a reward in return for giving is the idea of

reciprocity. In the context of relationships, and according to an article from MasterClass, healthy emotional reciprocity is a critical factor to prevent an unhealthy relationship, like when one person or people begin to feel used or unsupported.[16]

Reciprocity is a vital component to the balance of a successful relationship that is personal in nature, whether it is a friend, family member, coworker, or romantic partner. If we are intentionally working on healthy levels and a balance of empathy and power within ourselves, our relationships with others must be balanced and healthy as well. If Person A puts in all of the effort to make a relationship work, and feels as if their friend, family member (Person B), or partner does not put in an equal amount of effort, it is likely that they will distance themselves, or in the case of a romantic relationship, break up with them.

When it comes to ensuring relationships are balanced, it makes sense to ask the question, "What's in it for me? How does this relationship benefit me?" This is a question we can ask to gauge if the relationship is reciprocal or not. If we are constantly showing empathy to someone else without the same in return, it can become exhausting. At some point, you hold healthy power by setting boundaries at times for self-care and asking, "What's in it for me? Is this relationship still working?"

This is why self-care is critical in order to achieve balance with empathy within yourself as much as it is for others. We must take care of ourselves and be in check with how we feel in order to 1) have the energy to give to our relationships, and 2) know when we're giving energy to something that isn't worth it anymore. Two of the quotes that I live by and repeat often are: "If things aren't adding up, start subtracting" and "If you don't take care of yourself, you won't be strong enough to take care of anyone else." In this regard, asking about the WIIFM is relevant and necessary to be healthy and remain in balance for your own physical and mental health.

There are also times when asking "what's in it for me?" is not appropriate. There are many people who walk through life this way, constantly looking out for themselves first, and this outlook damages relationships, hurts other people, and comes with complete disregard for a sense of community, togetherness, and connectedness to others. At some point, we must be courageous enough to first give without confirming there is something for us to get out of it. This is why we might donate money or volunteer our time, or support a friend who is unable to give support back for a season. When we lead only with self, it can appear selfish to others and increase cultural misunderstandings, selfishness, and a mindset of just simply not caring about one another.

Both in our past and in our present, we have seen politicians, government officials, and non-governmental officials making decisions that are solely in their best interest with the purpose of seeking what's best for them. It is often under the guise that their decision was what was best for others, but usually that was a justification for their actions and did not involve empathy for all. Let me break this down even further.

There are people in government positions in local communities all the way up to the federal level in the House of Representatives, the Senate, and even in our court systems in all major political parties— Republican, Democratic, Libertarian, and independents—who are posing as leaders with balanced empathy and power, when in reality, they justify the use of their power or mask their use of power for their own personal or political gains. Fixing this in our political system and eliminating division means entrusting people to understand when leaders are not using a balance of empathy and power to guide their decisions for other people, and then act on making others aware and educated. This, by the way, should be the duty of being an elected official.

The only way to ensure people are placing leaders in office who are willing to operate within a balance of empathy and power is if the people are educated on what that looks like and how to act on it for themselves and for others. This is also rooted in understanding what power truly is (good and bad forms of it), how it manifests in different parts of our lives, and how to balance that with empathy. And have no fear, we are diving into power in the next chapter to help you learn and pass it on to others.

I have heard people say that the right thing is to always give to others more than you give to yourself. But the right thing could also be making sure you and your family are good before you give to others. What is the right thing to do?

If you never ask the question, "What's in it for me?" then this should be cause for reflection as you work to increase your inability to recognize, be aware of, acknowledge, and act on your own self-power. If you are constantly asking the question, "What's in it for me?" and ignoring the thoughts, feelings, and concerns of others, or not valuing the contributions of others, then that is cause for reflection, and it relates specifically to your inability to recognize that showing empathy and sharing power benefits everyone involved.

In the next chapter, I move this conversation towards power. Power is quite the energetic force, and when a person has a healthy balance between power and empathy, they will share the gift of unity, not division.

CHAPTER 3:
I Got The Power!

No, I am not talking about the song, "The Power" by SNAP... and if you know what that is, well then welcome to my brain. Instead, I'm discussing power—personal power like in the song, but perhaps not the house music dance party version.

Power has many definitions if you look it up in any dictionary. Here are the definitions from dictionary.com (2024):

+ The ability to do or act; capability of doing or accomplishing something
+ *Political* or national strength
+ The *possession* of *control* or *command over* people
+ *Political* ascendancy or *control* in the government of a country, state, etc.,
+ Legal ability, capacity, or *authority*
+ Delegated *authority; authority* granted to a person or persons in a particular office or capacity
+ A document or written statement conferring legal *authority*
+ A person or thing that *possesses* or exercises *authority* or influence
+ A particular form of mechanical or physical *energy* or *force*
+ The magnifying capacity of a microscope
+ A mathematical term[17]

The trend is clear. The words that are italicized are the words that appear over and over again in the definitions above: *control, authority, political, command,* and *force*. In this context, if I left out the scientific and mathematical meanings of the word, only political or governmental definitions of power would be left. Of course, there are other industries where power is held, but I think that the reason these two industries are directly mentioned is because when people in politics or government (law) use power, it not only has influence and control over whole groups and populations of people, but also control over how others' entire lives are lived.

Think of a person in power at your place of work or school—perhaps it's your boss, the CEO, the superintendent, the president of the college or university, etc. They have power over your work and your immediate surroundings. If they made an impactful decision, it would affect your work and, of course, parts of your life. However, those holding positions of power in a governmental or political office have the power to change the rights you have as a human being and how you must operate in your life and the lives of those around you. That is a LOT of control, authority, command, and force.

Interestingly, the above definitions are not the only ways in which power can be defined. I want to challenge you, in your work of balancing empathy and power, to *redefine* your definition of power. This is important because the traditional definitions of the word power are not all-encompassing of the ways in which power is used (or not) in a living human being. The traditional definitions are written in a way that accomplishes only power *over* another, but not always power *within* or power that benefits the whole. In this case, the whole simply means others and the community or society in which we live. How we use power, in balance with empathy, is one of the keys to unlocking division and building unity and community across America.

In new research performed by Larissa Conte, she defined thirty-six different types of power that exist in what she calls the "power landscape." Yes. Thirty-six.[18] Conte has spent her life's work researching the interconnectedness of human relationships and behavior to one another and how humans interact with one another. What is even more significant is these types of power do not just define power as it relates to control of/by others, they are also related to power in relationship with yourself. Conte has spent over twenty years as a global consultant, international executive coach, and has developed multiple courses after receiving her B.S. and M.S. from Stanford University in California. Her credibility along with her own personal growth in the field of power as leadership development are evident in her research outcomes.

Conte's definition of power is "the capacity to move energy through systems." Notice how the definition does not indicate power over, yet energy through a system. She states that the purpose of investigating the "power landscape" is to learn how to use power to serve the whole, or "power that sources from recognition of our interconnection used for the collective good of the community." She suggests that keeping "the whole" in mind can help direct how power should move in and out of each of the five spheres of the power landscape in a way that benefits others and ourselves in a healthy way.

The five spheres of the power landscape are:

+ Personal Wellbeing
+ Relationships and Intimacy
+ Organizational Transformation
+ Society and Nature
+ Ceremony and Meaning

Within each sphere, there are various types of power at work, which as previously mentioned totals to thirty-six types of power in all. Under each sphere is a list of six or more kinds of power within that sphere. These "powers" are neither good nor bad, just ways that energy moves. For example, in the sphere identified as powers related to personal wellbeing, we all have inner power, physical and emotional power, mental and sensing power, the power to learn, and the power to love. If we consider Conte's definition of power, which is "the capacity to move energy through systems," this means that inner power might be the capacity to move energy throughout ourselves. An example of this might be the power to create a dream and make it happen. Physical power could be defined as the capacity to use our physicality to move

Figure 1

WAYFINDING POWER LANDSCAPE

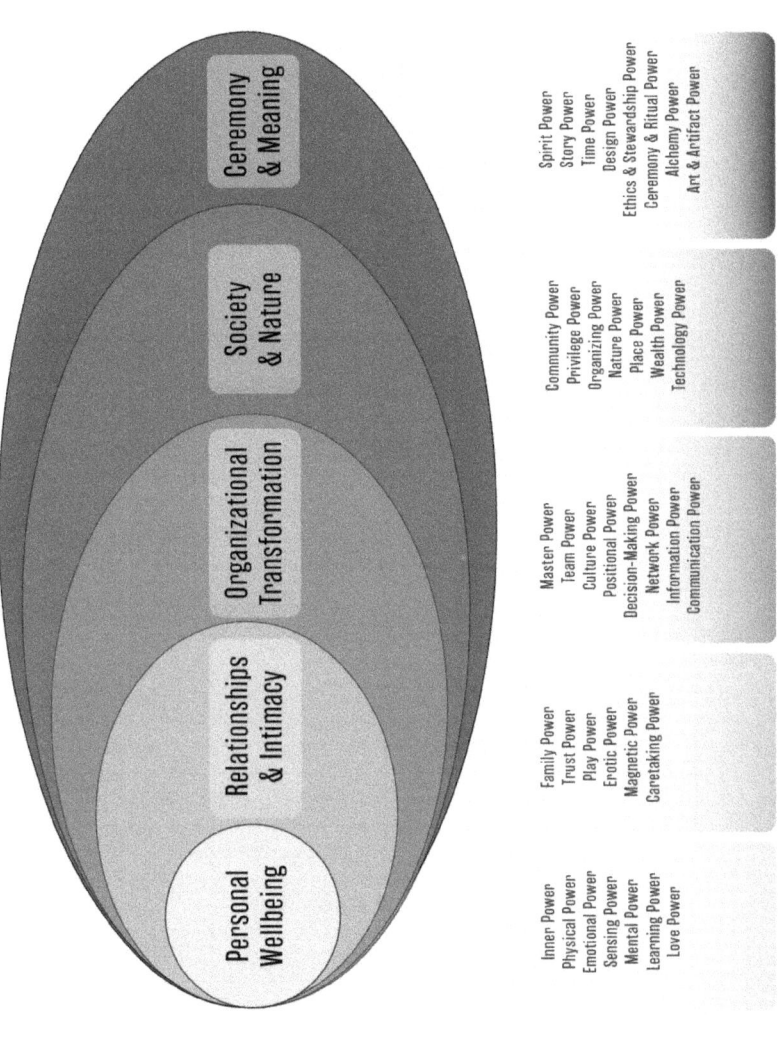

Personal Wellbeing

Relationships & Intimacy

Organizational Transformation

Society & Nature

Ceremony & Meaning

Inner Power
Physical Power
Emotional Power
Sensing Power
Mental Power
Learning Power
Love Power

Family Power
Trust Power
Play Power
Erotic Power
Magnetic Power
Caretaking Power

Master Power
Team Power
Culture Power
Positional Power
Decision-Making Power
Network Power
Information Power
Communication Power

Community Power
Privilege Power
Organizing Power
Nature Power
Place Power
Wealth Power
Technology Power

Spirit Power
Story Power
Time Power
Design Power
Ethics & Stewardship Power
Ceremony & Ritual Power
Alchemy Power
Art & Artifact Power

© 2023 Wayfinding, Inc.

energy through systems, like hiking our bodies up a mountain.

I had never experienced the thought of power as all-encompassing in every sphere of our lives, yet I had always thought of power as something people use for the common good or not (usually not). I definitely did not think power involved so much outside of the basic meanings of the definitions at the start of this chapter. In her coaching, Conte provides a power assessment that identifies areas of strength on a sliding scale and indicates where participants' power may be strong or needs improvement in the various areas. After receiving the results, she asks participants to examine each sphere separately to determine how that power manifests inside of the person individually, and then alternatively in the systems in which they work or go to school.

Out of the thirty-six types of power, there are twenty-four that show up more commonly in schools, businesses, and organizations:

	SPHERES OF INFLUENCE				
	Personal Wellbeing	Relationships & Intimacy	Organizational Transformation	Society & Nature	Ceremony & Meaning
TYPES OF POWER IN SCHOOLS, BUSINESSES, & ORGS.	Inner	Trust	Mastery	Privilege	Story
	Emotional	Caretaking	Positional	Community	Time
	Sensing	Play	Team	Organizing	Design
	Mental		Culture	Wealth	Ethics & Stewardship
	Learning		Network	Technology	
	Love		Information		
			Decision-Making		
			Communication		

 ## ACTIVITY: Examining Our Powers

As you think about these examples of power, think about how they can show up for you in your life, whether that is at work, school, or your individual relationships in those spaces. For example, mental power means how confident you are in your own mental ability related to intelligence or judgment. Trust power is related to how confident you are in trusting others and yourself. Learning power relates to your ability and willingness to learn new concepts and take in information, and then process it. Love power may be a surprise on this list, but it does not necessarily mean love in the context of romantic or intimate love. Instead, it refers to the ability to show acts of love and kindness towards others, or to act with love for another human.

Privilege power explains the power someone may have because of their own status. For example, if you are born into a family that has not had to worry about access to food, that is a privilege to have no anxiety over how you will find a way to eat. Team power is defined in the environment in which you feel you have the most power to work. Do you find that you have more power in a team versus working alone? These are all examples of how you may begin to investigate and define each type of power at work for yourself.

It is my suggestion that the types of power not listed here are more related to personal and romantic relationships and, while relevant to your own personal growth, are not appropriate for the workplace, community, or educational settings.

Grab a pen, pencil, or highlighter and note in the book, on a piece of paper, or on your device which of the twenty-four types of power you feel most strong in from the table.

For example, I might circle culture power, organizing power, inner power, and love power because I have spent a large part of my career working on culture within organizations, but also working with a wide variety of diverse cultures in humans. I would circle organizing power because in all of my professional experiences, I focused on organizational design and inherently have a desire for being organized. I am very intrinsically motivated and have a strong sense of self and purpose that contributes to my inner power, and the love I have for helping humans be better to one another, as well as the love I have for my children, family, and friends, fuels me forward.

Next, write down or circle/highlight with a different color which of the types of power above that you feel you are least confident in or could improve in. For example, I might circle technology power, wealth power, and design power. While I consider myself to be pretty savvy with computer software, when it comes to all technology or the inner workings of computers, engineering tech, writing code, or any of those things, my brain can't compute. While I do know that building wealth is important, when it comes to doing taxes or financial spreadsheets, I can't compute that either. I have some basic design skills, but I have a very hard time taking an abstract idea and turning it into something tangible, like graphic design or architecture, or creating things without a model. That is very difficult for my brain to do. I think you understand the ask now.

After you have identified strengths and areas of improvement, match them to their specific spheres and answer the following questions in your journal:

✦ Are there any patterns in the types of power I circled? For example: Do your strengths land in one specific sphere, or are they scattered across the spheres? What spheres do you have more strengths in vs. weaknesses, if any?

✦ After doing this activity and looking at the spheres your strengths and weaknesses lie in, what surprised you?

✦ Look at your strengths: What skills and experiences provide evidence of this type of power?

✦ Look at your areas of improvement: Are you avoiding doing additional work in these areas to improve your power, or could these areas be due to a lack of access to learning or professional development? Why might you feel like these are areas of improvement? Do you even feel the need to improve them?

If you are working in a team, discuss the following questions together:

✦ How can it help the team to know and identify the areas of power that each individual feels are their strengths?

✦ How can it help the team to know and identify the areas of power that each individual feels are their areas of improvement?

✦ What power types are most common among the team?

✦ What can the team do to keep power types in balance and hold each team member accountable? Or how might the team work to fill in talent or gaps in places that are not areas of strength?

✦ What spheres does the team need to improve upon?

If you are a professor or educator conducting this activity with a class of students, the above activities can be duplicated individually first, and then in small groups. I would not recommend doing the activity as a whole group or a full group share-out with students that may or may not see one another outside of a 50-minute class period. Some of this information may feel too personal for some to share.

Encourage students in small groups to lean into their personal power to get the most out of the activity. When they are finished, you may ask them how knowing this information can influence their ability to be a better leader in certain areas, or work to partner with others in their future careers.

When we evaluate our individual, group, and community manifestations of power, we can then find how to balance our strengths and weaknesses with *empathy*. When we are able to access empathy to imagine others' situations, pains, injustices, etc., we can then use our power to help ourselves and others, and in turn, heal division and disconnection.

Power does not have to be used in a manipulative fashion, yet it can coexist with empathy in a balanced way. As shown through Conte's work, the power to serve the whole can only exist if empathy is present. We don't know everyone's story, and we won't experience every symptom of the imbalance of empathy and power in the world personally. Empathy can help us channel others' experiences towards a better understanding of what others might need, and power helps us realize our courage and role in accomplishing behavioral changes to improve a sense of unity and eliminate division.

This does not mean that you are only serving others and that there is no permission granted to use power to serve yourself. The definition of power in the research and image above allows for a balance between power for self and power for the whole.

Shadow Power

Conte introduces a term called "Shadow Power." She defines it as "destructive, disconnecting power that is used to serve the individual ego or a small group of people at the expense of others."[20] The definition of "shadow power" is how some of us might define "power" in itself because we assume it always means power over another. Shadow power, then, is the opposite of power that serves the whole—it is power that serves the self. Conte indicates that all of us have shadow powers, and while they may not always manifest in a "bad" way, if coupled with negative experiences, they can become damaging and a tool that only serves the self. Conte goes on to say that it also arises when we operate from the illusion that we feel alone and think that our responsibility is only to our own needs and desires.

Shadow power exists whether we want it to or not, and in some cases, whether we are aware of it or not. In her course, Conte states that your shadow power patterns are a result of personal traumas, limiting and false beliefs, and sources of disconnection with the self and others.[21]

Knowing your shadow powers can lead you in a powerful direction because once you are aware of them, you are able to shift towards correction. Similarly, when we become aware of our biases, we can begin to correct those. In Figure 2 on the next page, you can see the spheres of influence and the powers that serve the self (shadow power) in each sphere, according to Conte.

For example, when I think about my personal wellbeing power sphere, I feel more empowered to help others and feel more alive when I am eating healthy, regularly exercising, and feeling mentally and emotionally strong. I feel more equipped to share positive energy with others, which is the power to serve the whole. On the contrary, it can be easy to fall into self-absorption when I focus too much on myself. I may start safeguarding my work and

Figure 2

SHADOW POWER LANDSCAPE

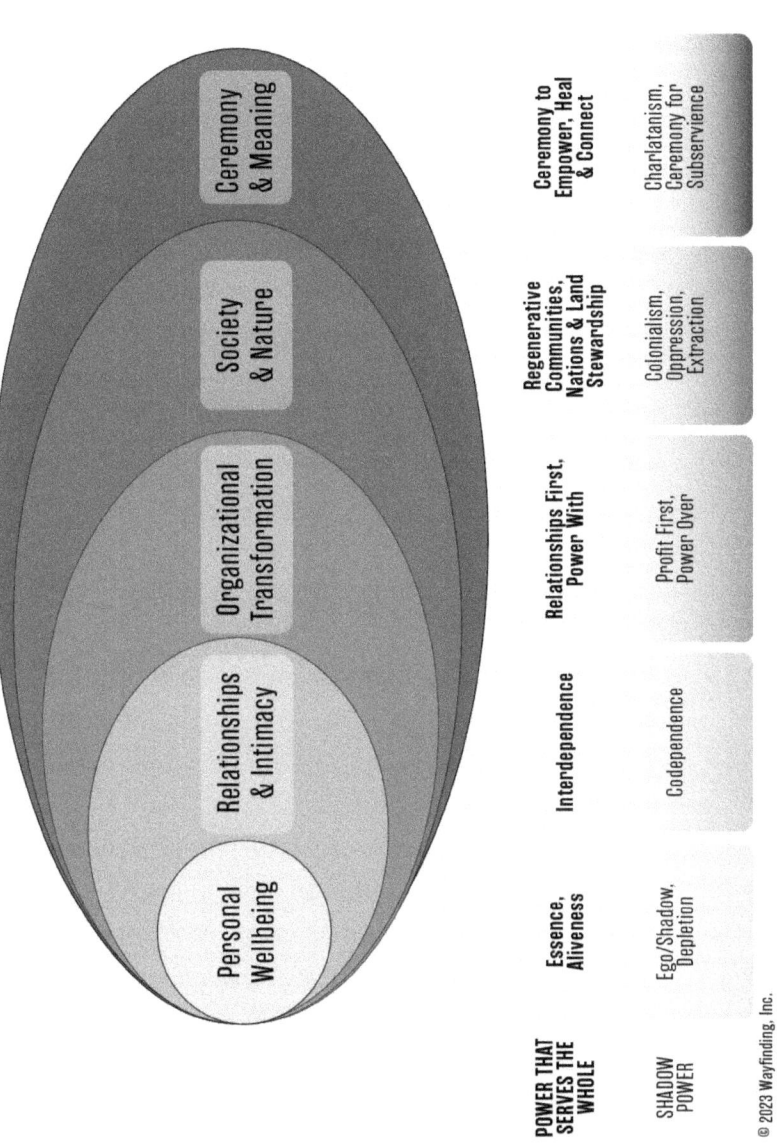

	Personal Wellbeing	Relationships & Intimacy	Organizational Transformation	Society & Nature	Ceremony & Meaning
POWER THAT SERVES THE WHOLE	Essence, Aliveness	Interdependence	Relationships First, Power With	Regenerative Communities, Nations & Land Stewardship	Ceremony to Empower, Heal & Connect
SHADOW POWER	Ego/Shadow, Depletion	Codependence	Profit First, Power Over	Colonialism, Oppression, Extraction	Charlatanism, Ceremony for Subservience

working in a silo, away from a team, or stop forming relationships with others who have different job or career paths because I feel they are beneath me if they aren't aspiring to leadership. I might become *too* protective of my mental health, blocking everyone from my vulnerabilities and therefore getting to know the real me. This is where power meant to serve the whole becomes a shadow power.

Shadow powers often take over when we are fueled by traumas and negative life experiences or living in a state of unhealth. For example, maybe a person is a leader, and they use the power of their network to get a promotional role over another person. In Corporate America, this may just feel like it is "just the way things work," and others may encourage you to work harder to build your network so that you can make the same types of moves up the corporate ladder. What is not taken into consideration in these situations is the harm this does to the overall system.

Conte calls this privilege power, which is often used to benefit the self and unintentionally cause harm to others who may have been more qualified yet did not get the opportunity to showcase skills and abilities. The types of moves described above are shadow powers manifesting as "power over," even though it may be justified as grit, hard work, and connections. Power that serves the whole prioritizes the person best fit for the job, regardless of status or connections of someone who is already in the business, who may be less qualified but more connected. If you have had personal feelings in opposition to blind resume's for example, that may be indicative of a shadow power related to privilege. Why would it bother you to know the candidate's name and appearance if their qualifications are the same?

The person who channels this power likely observed the practice of networking for promotion in other departments or in other role promotions across the business. It was a learned behavior that also models an unspoken cultural rule that ability is sometimes less important than whom you know. If that person gets the promotion over another who was more deserving based on work outcomes, then the person who did not land the promotion will either perpetuate the bias in the system or will distrust the procedures and systems. The outcome of shadow power is division and distrust in workplace culture, which is unhealthy, unjust, and poor business practice.

So the question then becomes, how do you discover your shadow areas? One way is to dive into Conte's work by accessing her free resources online or engaging with her directly and employing her executive coaching opportunities. Another way is to start with self-reflection.

Activity: Investigating Your Shadow Power

Grab your journal so that you can self-reflect about your shadow powers. You will have to be honest and open to self-reflection and constructive feedback from others to complete this exercise. It can cause some anxiety, but it will be paramount to your personal and professional growth.

1.   Read your own responses to the questions you answered about power on page 58. Specifically, look at the answers to your questions about the power types in which you felt most confident.

2.   As you analyze your responses, identify whether your answer indicated a power to serve the whole (self and community) or if the responses only served you, your ego, or a smaller group of people, like your personal family and friends.

3.   If you uncover an area where you feel confident in your power, but only serves the self, ego, or seems disconnected from community, what motivations, thoughts, or feelings cause you to act in this way?

4.   Now, identify three to four people in your life who will be honest with you regarding the various spheres of the power landscape. Perhaps it is your spouse or partner (Relationships and Intimacy sphere), your manager or close colleague (Organizational Transformation sphere), your friend (Society and Nature sphere), and a person with spiritual knowledge about you (Ceremony and Meaning sphere).

5.   Ask your selected people if they have ever observed your confidence in any of the thirty-six types of power (or the types of power linked to the sphere their relationship to you falls under) in

ways that did not serve the whole, yet only served you, your ego, or a smaller group of people.

  a. Do their thoughts align with yours? How do they compare? Differ?

  b. Did you identify a trend across the conversations with others?

  c. How does that make you feel?

  d. What can you do differently?

6.   After having these discussions, review your notes. Based on your findings and insights of yourself and what other perceptions were, identify three areas of improvement regarding your power and shadow powers, and three areas of personal strength that you think would make the largest impact in your life and in the lives of those around you if you honed in on (including your community and the physical environment).

Shadow Powers and Trauma

When I participated in Conte's course, and she guided us to reflect on our shadow power, I found shadow areas emerging in my life that consisted of the following: judgment and criticism of others in my ego, codependence, and power over others. I found this because I have always felt confident in my professional life, but sometimes that confidence manifested in only thinking of myself in my earlier career. At various points along my professional growth, and after participating in assessments that allowed others to share their insights and perceptions, there were times when I used my power over others through ego or simply through the use of authority. In my personal life, however, I had a strong reliance on relationships, which led to me giving some of my power away.

As stated, Conte describes shadow power origins in potential traumas, and I have had my fair share of life hardships. I have encountered divorce, two major career shifts, traumas from other failed relationships, a significant amount of death of family members and others in a short period of time, illness, racial and gender-based discrimination, and two life-threatening experiences for me and my own child.

The process of uncovering how those events affected the way I thought and communicated was enlightening, scary and life changing. All of the professional career decisions I have made have been rooted in a gut calling to help others, to communicate and model the importance of accepting all, and to dismantle division. You could imagine my surprise in doing these exercises when I discovered that there were also instances of blocking positive use of my power, using power to hold grudges and anger, and not allowing power to manifest positively to benefit not only the whole but also myself.

For example, somewhere along the journey of my life, I stopped wanting to spend time outside. I have always been passionate about doing the right thing for our planet. I still get anxious and frustrated when I see trash in the middle of the street, or people not recycling, or when I see forests cleared on long road trips. For some reason, I have always felt a strong, energetic connection to trees. I love trees—tropical trees like palms, majestic trees like the sequoias, deciduous trees like the big oak trees in my area of the country, and unique trees like the willow tree. I actually have a photo of me hugging a tree on a weekend trip to Virginia. Quite literally, I am a tree hugger. At some point, however, I stopped going outside to be around them. I felt a powerful connection with nature and was comfortable and confident when I was outside engaging in nature walks, sitting in parks, or just having fun being outdoors. And then, over time, my relationship with nature started to change because I became extremely focused on myself as a result of life circumstances.

I have now realized that the lack of connection led me to a shadow power in the power sphere of Society and Nature, and more specifically, the power type: Nature Power. Life started getting very busy. I was traveling a lot for work, my mom, who had been battling Alzheimer's for over a decade, was nearing the end of her fight, the pandemic happened, I gained weight, and I was alone. I hadn't reached a state of depression necessarily, but I definitely had gotten to a point where I just started to feel like "What's the point of doing anything extra?" I was on autopilot and spending most of my time indoors.

I also lived in the part of the U.S. that has a cicada emergence every seventeen years. It just so happened that right after COVID-19 shut down the world, the cicadas appeared in record numbers. Then I really was NOT going outside at a time when that was really all that anyone could do outside of their homes. At that point, I had convinced myself that I didn't like to be outside at all. I stopped wanting to have potlucks outside, stopped taking nature walks, and stopped doing anything outside if trees were involved.

During the discovery phase of investigating the ways in which my power moves through systems, I took a trip to New Orleans. Oh, how I love NOLA. The incredible food, the sounds of live jazz and blues, and all other types of music, the beignets, the art and culture, the history, the stories of the people, and well, I would be remiss not to mention the drink of choice lovingly and strategically called The Hurricane. New Orleans leads you to the streets, and you just get pulled in by all of it. On this trip, I finally had the time to walk leisurely, observing no time limits, itineraries, or schedules. I wandered into one of the many art stores just past Café du Monde in the French Quarter. It was tucked behind the storefronts on Decatur Street. Dutch Alley Artists Co-op is what it was called, and it is still there today.

As I walked around looking at all of the gorgeous visual art, I was amazed to find out that a few of the artists were in-house creating art in the store. It was just as mesmerizing as the sounds of New Orleans with the smell of beignets drifting in the door. I purchased a little art token and turned to leave, and then as I walked to the front door, I felt this urge to look up to see the art that was placed a little higher on the right wall just before walking out. I wouldn't say it was a voice because I didn't hear voices. It was just this feeling of making sure I had seen everything before I left. And like magic, it was a picture of a tree with a poem written around it by Walt Whitman.

I stopped in my tracks and walked over to get a closer view, but it was so high on the wall that the glare from the sunlight pouring into the art store was obstructing my ability to see the words clearly. I kindly asked one of the artists to take it down for me to get a closer look. As the kind man was coming down from the step ladder, art in hand, he said, "This one caught your eye, huh? I thought you were heading out the door!" I chuckled, and I said, "Something about it pulled me in! I love trees!" To which he responded, "Well, I'm the artist on this one! I used an ink press from the actual wood of the trees and other artifacts to create the stencils. This was made from a Louisiana tree, and the poem just seemed to fit!" I was very honored to meet him and thanked him for sharing that information.

He left me to take in the poem, and as I read it, tears welled in my eyes. Before I knew it, I was sobbing in the middle of the art store, and I couldn't stop myself. The poem reads:

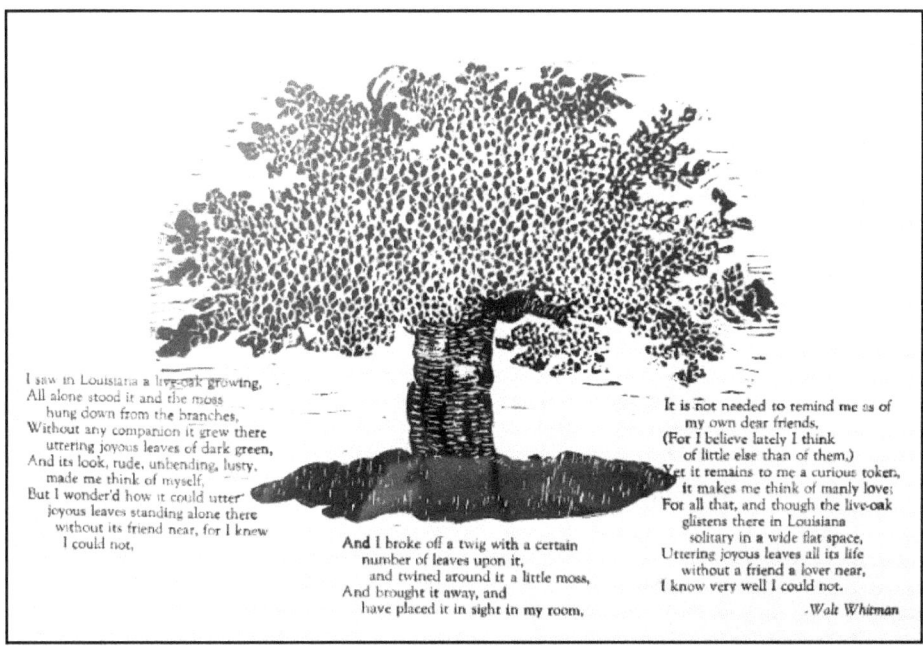

I saw in Louisiana a live-oak growing,
All alone stood it and the moss
    hung down from the branches,
Without any companion it grew there
    uttering joyous leaves of dark green,
And its look, rude, unbending, lusty,
    made me think of myself,
But I wonder'd how it could utter
    joyous leaves standing alone there
    without its friend near, for I knew
    I could not,

And I broke off a twig with a certain
    number of leaves upon it,
    and twined around it a little moss,
And brought it away, and
    have placed it in sight in my room,

It is not needed to remind me as of
    my own dear friends,
(For I believe lately I think
    of little else than of them,)
Yet it remains to me a curious token,
    it makes me think of manly love;
For all that, and though the live-oak
    glistens there in Louisiana
    solitary in a wide flat space,
Uttering joyous leaves all its life
    without a friend a lover near,
I know very well I could not.

.Walt Whitman

Art By John Fitzgerald

HEALING DIVISION

I saw in Louisiana a live-oak growing,
All alone stood it, and the moss
hung down from the branches,
Without any companion it grew there
uttering joyous leaves of dark green,
And its look, rude, unbending, lusty,
made me think of myself,
But I wonder'd how it could utter
joyous leaves standing alone there
Without its friend near, for I knew
I could not,

And I broke off a twig with a certain
number of leaves upon it,
and twined around it a little moss,
And brought it away, and
have placed it in sight in my room,

It is not needed to remind me as of
My own dear friends,
(For I believe lately I think
of little else than of them.)
Yet it remains to me a curious token,

it makes me think of manly love;
For all that, and though the live-oak
glistens there in Louisiana
solitary in a wide flat space,
Uttering joyous leaves all its life
without a friend a lover near,
I know very well I could not.

- *Walt Whitman*

I have never read a poem that resonated so deeply with my thoughts and feelings, especially based on where I was in life at that exact moment.

I started to investigate how my life experiences had affected me in ways I had not realized. The picture of the tree is what initially drew me in to read the poem, because despite my distance from nature, my love for trees never waned. It was my engagement with trees in nature that subsided over time, and when I read the poem about the tree feeling alone "without any companion" at times uttering "joyous leaves" and the author describing how he could not find joy in standing alone, it just resonated. Had I not been open to investigation at that time of my life, the picture of the tree would not have drawn me in, and I would not have had such a profound moment in the middle of an art store in Louisiana about a tree in Louisiana made from a tree in Louisiana. Needless to say, I did the best I could to wipe my eyes, and I walked straight to the counter to purchase the picture. It hangs on the wall next to my desk to remind me that neither the tree nor me will ever be alone now. I became reconnected to "going outside" after that.

The power and energy that flowed through that experience was life-changing because it dismantled the division I had created between me and the physical environment itself. I had been exercising a shadow power by extracting myself from nature power. In the reflection of my own life, my experiences, and the various types of power, I was able to recognize the shadow power that surfaced unknowingly.

It is important to remember that power can manifest in multiple ways, and removing certain forms of power (like nature) from your life, or attempting to ignore pieces of power, may not have a detrimental effect on others, but it can have a detrimental effect on you. Over time, this can take a negative toll on your ability to make a difference in multiple aspects of your life or through your leadership, whether it be in professional or personal ways. The goal is balance in all things when it comes to empathy and power, and that includes your own inner balance. To make positive changes in behavior as a leader, and more importantly, just as a human, take the time to dig into self-reflection in a healthy way through the exercises in the chapters above to step outside of yourself and see the gaps and the shadows.

These exercises are hard and time consuming work and are an important way to begin to recognize how you use power in your own life as well as determine if you are using that power to serve the whole or operating in your shadow power and using that power only for serving the self (in other words, disconnection at the expense of others). Investigating power and shadow power is one step towards healing divisions that you don't even realize you are creating. You are already becoming a part of the solution.

CHAPTER 4:
The Dark Side: Power Abuse

"No, Luke, I am your father." One of the most popular movie lines from the 1980s was delivered by James Earl Jones, the voice and actor behind one of the most popular movie villains of all time, Darth Vader, in the movie *The Empire Strikes Back* (1980).[22] I am a huge *Star Wars* fan. In fact, every Christmas Eve morning, in a family tradition created years ago with my two boys, we don our sweats and PJs, and choose a movie to see together in the theatres. For several amazing years, we were often awaiting the next Star Wars movie in the original saga to be released so we could see it together on Christmas Eve morning. For those who are not Star Wars fans, here is a very short summary of how Darth Vader came to be one of the largest and most well-known villains in movie history.

The movie is set on various planets in the universe, and the basic plot line, like most successful movies, is centered on the good vs. evil theme. In the film, there are space militaries that battle it out in the skies for a variety of reasons. There are animal-like characters who speak, some who speak different planetary languages based on where they are located in the galaxy, and human characters who speak English.

Anakin Skywalker was a young slave boy from the planet Tatooine (pronounced Tatoo-een. I can't have you repeating this information to sound cool at your next Christmas party, and you say the names incorrectly), and he was about nine or ten years old. He was a kid genius, building robots from scrap parts, maneuvering around the landscape, and was an amazing pilot. He was identified by a Jedi Knight, who became his mentor and friend, Obi-Wan Kenobi (pronounced Obee-wahn Ken-oh-bee).

He left Tatooine with Obi-Wan to study how to become a Jedi Knight and left his mother behind. Although he wasn't there, using his Jedi powers he could sense that she was in danger. He missed his mother and later found out that an evil army came and destroyed the town, and she was killed. It haunted him in his dreams often. Later, he reconnected with a beautiful woman whom he had previously met when he was just a boy. She was now the Queen of a different planet, Queen Padme Amidala (pronounced Pad-may Ah-mi-dah-luh) from Naboo. A young man, now, Ani, going by the nickname he was given by his Jedi friends, fell in love with the Queen. Their love and relationship were very secret because she was royalty, and he was essentially a member of the Jedi Knights at that time. It was against the rules for him to be involved with her. They secretly wed, and she became pregnant with twins.

Anakin was still haunted by the loss of his mother, and he feared the loss of Padme and his two children. He began having dreams about her dying or struggling in childbirth and feared that they would also lose their babies. He began to sense it again with his Jedi abilities. When his dreams occurred, they were seen as visions or premonitions of the future. He was becoming increasingly conflicted and emotional. It wasn't long before he had a meeting with a Dark Lord, who was hiding his true identity, pretending to be a good guy as a member of the Senate. The Senate was the governing body of the universe, where each planet or designated universal location was given an elected seat to make decisions. You might compare it to the United Nations global summits. Anakin trusted him and did not know that he was the Dark Lord at this point. However, this Dark Lord was hiding who he really was and his motivations. When the Dark Lord sensed the hate, fear, and anger inside of Anakin due to the loss of his mother and the fear of losing Padme, he revealed his true powers and identity to Anakin, and began to manipulate Anakin's emotions and told him that if he came "to the Dark Side" to fight with him that he would assume enough power and strength to save Padme from death.

In a very emotional battle, Obi-Wan, Anakin's teacher and protege, was forced to battle Anakin once he had transitioned fully to the dark side. Obi-Wan defeated Ani and left him to die in volcanic lava flows, but without Obi-Wan's awareness, Anakin was rescued by the Dark Lord, identified as Darth Sidious, who saved Anakin's life using robotic materials, armor, and a permanent oxygen mask helmet. Darth Vader, formerly Anakin Skywalker, was born.

As it turned out, Padme did die during childbirth, but the twin babies were delivered safely and lived. Their survival was kept hidden from the Dark Side and from Anakin (now Darth Vader since he turned to the dark side) because the Jedi wanted the children to grow up safely. The twins, Luke and Leia, were split up into different families to be cared for, with the random watchful eye of Obi-Wan Kenobi in the shadows. Not even Luke and Leia knew that they had a brother or sister, let alone a twin out in the universe.

Many years later, Luke was approached by Jedi Knights who indicated he should fight for the Republic (the "good" army of men and women who were fighting to save others and maintain peace) and also be trained as a Jedi. You see, Luke had incredible pilot skills that he inherited from his father, Anakin. He ended up being sent away to train for the Jedi, much like his father, and eventually started flying a fighter starship jet for the Republic. As he proved himself to be very skilled, he eventually came face-to-face with the dark side leader, Darth Vader. It was Darth Vader who realized something was different about the "force" and the feelings he felt when he was around Luke. Later, he discovered the truth: Luke was his son. He confronted Luke and told him the truth.

Darth tried to convince Luke to join him as father and son on the Dark Side and brought him to the Sith Lord to "complete his journey to the dark side." In this iconic scene, the audience can sense that Darth Vader is beginning to feel conflicted about bringing Luke to see the Sith Lord, and he starts to appear more human again—more like his "good side" – more like Anikan. Luke begins to fight Darth Vader in front of the Sith Lord as the Sith Lord encourages Luke to use his feelings of anger to fuel his strength in the Dark Side as he battles Darth Vader, his father.

In the middle of the fight, Luke begins to evade his father, Darth Vader.

Rather than fight him, he starts to run and hide rather than face him again in another battle.

Luke says, "Your thoughts betray you, father. I feel the good in you, the conflict. You couldn't bring yourself to kill me before, and I don't believe you'll destroy me now."

Darth Vader continues to fight his feelings and battle Luke to prove his loyalty to the Sith Lord, and it is in this battle that he discovers that Luke has a sister.

Darth threatens Luke by saying, "If you will not submit to the Dark Side, then perhaps she will."

This angers Luke as he jumps out of his hiding place, because he now feels a sense of protection over his sister, Leia, and he starts fighting his father once again. As they continue to fight, Luke eventually disarms Darth Vader and cuts off his hand at the wrist with the ever-famous lightsaber sword, leaving Darth Vader defenseless and vulnerable. The Sith Lord descends a set of stairs, cloaked in a long black hooded cape, his face old and almost corpse-like with hollow eyes.

He says to Luke with an evil chuckle, "Good. Your hate has made you powerful. Now, fulfill your destiny and take your father's place at my side."

Luke stops and throws the disarmed lightsaber to the ground and refuses to join the Dark Side, stating, "I am a Jedi, like my father before me."

The Sith Lord replies, "So be it, Jedi. You will die." The Sith Lord begins torturing Luke. Because he was a powerful Dark Lord, he electrocuted Luke as bolts of lightning shot from his hands, causing a slow, painful death. The camera begins to pan over to Darth Vader, who is constantly looking back and forth between the Sith Lord and Luke and back again. In a stunning reversal, Darth Vader, now returning to his true inner self as Anakin, begins to walk towards the Sith Lord, who is electrocuting Luke as lightning bolts shoot out of his hands and around his body. Darth Vader picks up the Sith Lord while being electrocuted himself and drops him over the edge of the spaceship and into the vastness of the universe. He immediately drops to his knees, and Luke runs to him. Darth Vader has returned to Anakin and has saved Luke's life.

Luke tries to carry his dad to safety, but Anakin is just too weak. He asks

Luke to take off his mask, and he dies looking at Luke in the eyes. Because Anakin used love towards his only son to defeat the dark side, he regained his status as a good person in the movie, as love and kindness defeated the Dark Side inside of him. The audience is left feeling empathy and compassion for Luke and for his father. You see, it was hatred and fear combined with the Sith Lord's ability to use the emotional trauma that Anakin had faced to fuel his fear and anger into an even darker place. True unconditional love for his family brought him back into the same place of love and peace, which he used selflessly to save his son.

You may be wondering why I chose to start this chapter with a summary of a fictional character in a sci-fi make-believe world. While this is an exaggerated fictional account, it is a perfect example of what happens when the desire for power is used for self at the expense of others. It is also an example of how hate, fear, and anger fuel the need for power, manipulation, control, and division. This is power abuse. In the sections that follow in this chapter, I examine how the shadow powers that you read about in the previous chapter can manifest to create division and cause oppressive systems across the world, and on a smaller scale, can create division on teams, in businesses, organizations, schools, and more.

Power Over Another

As you now know, shadow powers exist for all forms of power and can emerge or take over at any point, when triggered by stress. Remember that we can all access power consciously or involuntarily and learning more about ourselves helps us identify the times we may slip into our shadow powers. For example, one might have "inner power," with a strong sense of self, intuition, and trust in themselves. However, this could quickly turn into a shadow power driven by ego and serving the self if not checked, or if a person is living in an unhealthy mental state.

Many of us find ourselves in situations throughout the course of our lives where someone has power over us and they use that power to serve themselves. There are times when this power exerted over us is out of our control, and there are other times when people willingly give their power away as a result of their own previous traumas or fears.

Sometimes, people in powerful positions of leadership use their power to benefit only themselves and/or those whom they deem worthy of receiving the benefits of their power. An example of a historical figure that most people are aware of is Adolf Hitler. It is a harsh and extreme example, but it is a clear example of someone who held a powerful position of leadership and used that power over others to fatally harm over 30 million people. His motivations were self-centered, not centered on serving the whole, although he characterized and justified it differently.

Because this is such a highly sensitive and horrific topic to discuss, this information is not meant to excuse any of the abhorrent behavior by Hitler or those who carried out his orders. It is to provide information and insight into what people may not know about some of the backstory of Hitler's early life as an example of what can lead people into exerting control over others.

Hitler reportedly had a very difficult time in the German military during World War I when he was young. He was brutalized for four years in the trenches and left the war wounded and temporarily blinded. When he returned home, Germany was more progressive. It was a "forerunner of modernity in virtually every field" at that time, and he did not agree with the "new republic" after returning from WWI. He wanted to go back to the "Old Germany." Unfortunately, he was convinced that the groups of people responsible for the new, modern German Republic were anyone who didn't agree with the old Republic, and people of the Jewish faith.[23]

Hitler, rather than feeling safe with those meant to support him after the war, felt vulnerable and unprotected. He likely suffered from what we now know is PTSD or post-traumatic stress disorder. As a result, he made it his life's mission to use his influence, shadow powers, and intelligence to seek political power over entire populations of people to eliminate them, even if they were not the cause of his original traumas.

He was also reportedly paranoid about health as well throughout his life, somewhat of a hypochondriac, and suffered from some psychosis due to the almost 60 medications he routinely took, not long before taking his own life.

There were reports that he had an addiction to opiates. A former leader of the Central Intelligence Agency (CIA) commissioned a top-secret report based on psychoanalysis and statements from Hitler's close allies. It stated that he suffered from hysteria, paranoia, and schizophrenia, indicating potential undiagnosed mental health conditions. All of these are examples of what have been characterized as key contributors to the abuse of power by researchers.

There are several reasons why people who gain power over others lean into their shadow powers, using and abusing this power. In my experiences and research, I have found that the core reasons for abusing power are usually centered on one or more of the following:

+ Previous life trauma
+ Mental health conditions
+ Fear of loss of a person or financial stability
+ Addiction

Previous Life Traumas and Mental Health Conditions

Sometimes, previous life traumas and some mental health conditions can lead to an abuse of power or power that is used to serve the self. If someone never receives help or heals from their previous traumas, they can sometimes account for that by attempting to control every aspect of their lives or of those around them. Creating and maintaining this control helps them feel safe and limits outside variables from creeping into their lives and catching them off guard. It is an attempt to limit the triggering of their own anxieties or fears because of their trauma or potential condition. As we read about power previously, control is an application of the abuse of power.

In Chapter 3 of *Understanding the Impact of Trauma*, it is discussed that people who have experienced trauma and do not receive treatment for it, or who do not create healthy coping skills to heal from it, can suffer from the following: a loss of hope for the future, anxiety, agitation, dissociation or confusion, emotional detachment or numbing, beliefs that emotional expression is too dangerous and leads to a lack of control, and depression.[24] The reason is that during times of stress, our brains release hormones and signals that shut down the part of the brain whose purpose is to make executive decisions. The brain, when under periods of stress, conserves energy and perceives an attack, so it only sends out signals to fight or run away, which is what we call "fight or flight." The brain is operating at a limited capacity when this happens. If someone never heals from their trauma and leans into control and power abuse, they often feel this fight or flight feeling, and their decision-making abilities are compromised. This also exemplifies an imbalance of empathy and power because the original source of thought beings with the self.

In my research of people who have abused power and affected others (which includes larger populations of people as well), I found they have often experienced one or more of the following:

+ Physical or mental abuse by a family member
+ Repeated rejection and isolation
+ Financial hardships early in life
+ Experienced the tragic death of a family member or loved one
+ Symptoms of mental health conditions (i.e., bipolar disorder, paranoia, Narcissistic Personality Disorder, OCD, etc.)

It is difficult to cope and move past these deeply harmful and personal experiences, and The University of Rochester Neuroscience team explains why. They state that your brain is actually "rewired" after a traumatic event.[25] Traumatic events actually physically change the ability of your brain to make sound decisions and can cause conflict in the brain's emotional centers. Your brain actually begins to argue with itself, in layman's terms. This is one of the reasons why it has been regarded as a healthy practice not to make major life decisions in periods of stress or make any major decisions at work that can have lasting effects on the business, employees, or customers.

In some cases, extended trauma that happens as a child can manifest in unhealthy ways as an adult, particularly for boys. In the medical journal article, "The Cycle of Abuse: When Victims Become Offenders," Plummer and Cossins argue that a cycle of abuse (or the abuse of power) is more likely to continue due to the following four factors:

1. Normalization of violence and abuse: This occurs when the abuse occurs for so long that it becomes normalized as a way of life. People in this scenario then feel abnormal when the abuse is absent.

2. Disempowerment and lack of control: This occurs when the victim of abuse has felt a loss of control for so long that they overcompensate for this and later seek to regain control by using dominance over others.

3. Sexualization of aggression: This occurs when the victim has experienced sexual abuse, and it leads to confusion about the connections between intimacy, power, and emotion.

4. Lack of support and intervention: This occurs when the victim is left without support or proper intervention of healthy strategies to cope with the mental anguish from the abuse, and therefore leads to harmful behaviors of self or others.[26]

There are leaders in positions of power that may be abusing their power because of one or more of these researched and identified reasons. When we lose control in our lives or over what happens to us and do not have the innate ability, healthy support systems, or accountability partners who can identify unhealthy patterns or behaviors, an imbalance of empathy and power is the result. When leaders abuse others or their authority because of trauma, without intervention, they continue ongoing cycles of power abuse. This is when power is used to serve the self or harm others as a shadow power, instead of power that is used to serve the whole. If the goal of leadership is to use power to help others and for the overall health of a business, organization, or society, then self-control and operating from a healthy brain are extremely important. As you can now identify from the research, the alternative can be exceedingly detrimental.

Fear of Loss of a Person or Financial Stability

Fear is quite a motivator and not always a healthy one. Leading with fear as a tool of manipulation, control, and power over someone is effective. It works. We would hate to admit that, but it is a tried-and-true mechanism that is still working in homes, schools, sports teams, businesses, and churches, on leadership teams, government, and even in yourself. I can't tell you how many times I have heard a parent say, "I put the fear of God in them." I hate to admit smiling when I hear the line from a dad in an old sitcom when he says to his son, "I brought you into this world, and I'll take you out." When you dissect that statement, it's pretty terrifying to essentially threaten the fear of death for not doing something the parent deems appropriate. The fact that I smiled and laughed at it is because we may have heard our own parents say it. I was lucky to know that my parents never meant it literally - they would never have harmed me, and I am grateful for that. But when they said it, I knew it was time for me to stop doing whatever it was that I was doing.

Unfortunately, there are some parents who do mean it literally, and that is a level of fear that is not funny. Not at all. Fear is powerful because as we read previously, fear paralyzes parts of the brain and the brain perceives fear as a threat to our personal wellbeing, even if that fear is not a physical threat of harm. When the brain perceives a threat, it reacts in the same way as if there were a physical threat in front of us.

In an article in *The New Yorker* titled, "Is it Anxiety, or Is a Tiger Trying to Kill You?" Kathryn Kvas details a satirical example of anxiety, stating, "to help patients understand anxiety, therapists often compare it to being chased by a tiger, since anxiety was originally an early defense mechanism against predators. That's why it causes things like heightened fear, tunnel vision, and loss of bowel control. (Yikes! Bodies are interesting, huh?)"[27] Fear causes anxiety, which causes the same fight or flight response that was discussed. It shuts down our ability to think with our entire brain, and instead, we make rash decisions that are not well thought out most of the time. Recall, when people experience anxiety, they feel a lack of control and they attempt to exert that control over themselves and others to minimize those feelings. Anxieties are emotional and relate to several aspects of our modern lives. Chronic financial hardship is one of these emotional triggers. Financial hardships in early life as a future factor of power over another may be more of an indirect and confusing connection to some. I want to be clear about what financial hardship means because it is different for everyone. Fear, anxiety and stress related to financial hardship is dependent upon how someone perceives what not having "enough" means to them, and this could be realized as feeling a lack of physical safety, if the hardship results in being homeless or living in an unsafe neighborhood. It could also be from remembering extreme physical symptoms of hunger because there wasn't ever enough food, money for food, or cramped spaces because there were multiple people in a small living space growing up, or always being alone because of possible neglect due to the lack of being able to afford child care. There are numerous fears and anxieties that are a result of not having enough money. Financial abuse is another way people are harmed in controlling relationships whether personal or professional (think budget control or blocking pay raises if professional). This is just another way power can be misused and out of balance with empathy.

The fear of loss of a person is also a paralyzing emotion and can be used to manipulate if there is a threat to someone else's livelihood. This may seem like an extreme scenario for the workplace, but indirectly, the same feelings exist. Imagine a boss or supervisor who makes a statement like, "If you can't figure out how to handle your own childcare coverage, then we are going to have to let you go." The boss says this without knowing that the stability of your life is in question without the job, which means the potential loss of your spouse or partner. There are also people who have already lost family members or people close to them, and the fear of potentially losing another person triggers the brain towards a constant state of fight or flight.
These are all symptoms of the root emotion, which is fear.

There are a multitude of emotions and thoughts that can lead to never wanting to feel that way again. Some humans in that position may go to extremes to ensure they do not find themselves in positions to feel fear or anxiety in their adult lives, and those extreme measures may involve maintaining power over their own life or someone else in order to secure it, just like Anakin Skywalker. It aligns with Plummer and Cossin's research above related to feeling disempowered or a lack of control and the desire to regain that control by any means necessary even if it means abusing power.

Addiction

Addiction can be a controversial subject in and of itself because some people within the scientific community argue that addiction is a behavioral problem, while others believe it is a hereditary brain disease passed from generation to generation. *The New York Times* reports that, unlike diseases of the brain like Alzheimer's or the effects of COVID-19, personal choice does play a role in both starting and ending drug and alcohol use. As we examine addiction further, there are several reasons why people may choose to use a substance like drugs or alcohol, but the majority of them revolve around the following reasoning:

✦ To forget something that caused harm in the past, whether emotional or physical,
✦ To numb pain,
✦ The fear of being left out or peer pressure, or
✦ The belief that the substance will help them perform better at work or in school (this is related to some of the prescription medications that enhance focus, but also have addictive properties when overused or used improperly).[28]

The root of these reasons is usually some sort of fear, anxiety, or trauma, which can all lead to addiction and, later, power abuse. The interesting nuance with addiction is that if we subscribe to the belief that addiction is both behavioral and biological, then those who are predisposed to addictive personalities can also become addicts of anything that has addictive properties, not just illegal substances or alcohol. For example, think of how many people you may know, it may even be you, who stops to get lottery tickets or someone that becomes addicted to the rush of winning when gambling. While the method used is a choice, the addictive predisposition may already be present and the person has a difficult time stopping that behavior.

Let's look at addiction through the lens of business and leadership. In the article, "Why Does Power Abuse Persist?" Sean Peek writes that 28 million workers have been bullied on the job by someone who outranks them in the organization's hierarchy.[29] Power abuse in the workplace causes toxic work environments and damages employee morale and relationships due to people exploiting their authority and positional power (see diagram on pg. 55) Sometimes, the power abuse continues and others around them actually encourage it because the workplace culture may be designed to exist in this manner. The question still remains: why does this abuse even occur, and why so often in the workplace?

According to research in "On Power and Its Corrupting Effects: The Effects of Power on Human Behavior and the Limits of Accountability Systems," Tobore examined the effects of power through an integrated synthesis of neurological, sociological, physiological, and psychological literature and scientific studies. Tobore found that power can dramatically change ordinary people's behavior, causing them to abuse it and therefore make poor decisions. He added that "evidence suggests that in efforts to avoid power loss, powerful people may be willing to use coercion and go to extra lengths at the expense of others."[30] *This is because power addiction causes the same physiological response as any other addiction:* the release of dopamine into the bloodstream.

Dopamine is what some call the "feel good hormone"—a neurotransmitter made in your brain and is a chemical messenger of sorts. It can also act like a hormone and is released along with other hormones in the kidneys and in the back of your brain. When you do something that your body perceives as pleasurable, large amounts of dopamine are released, giving you a feeling of happiness and relief. When someone receives power, they can become addicted to it, needing more and more. This is why we often see people in power rise to levels of dictatorship—the power they have isn't enough, and they need more. For whatever reason, being in control of others has led to a strong dopamine release that must be chased to no end.

Addiction is a shadow power that exists in the sphere of relationships as codependence (Conte). It is listed as codependence because the person abusing and addicted to power is dependent on the need for that power in order to feel good and comfortably exist. In other words, without power, the person addicted to power feels worthless, depressed, and unable to function properly, like someone who is codependent on other people or a substance. In contrast, when you serve the whole for the benefit of others and yourself and are in balance with power, you are interdependent. Interdependence is the interaction and collaboration of everyone working together to balance their power and empathy.

Fear + Isolation + Separation = Maintain Control

Fear, isolation, and separation are the nails in the coffin to maintain control and power over others. Fear is a mechanism for power over others because it turns on the signal in the brain to shut down all other decision-making abilities. You are no longer operating with a full, thoughtful brain. Isolation and separation must follow fear to keep people feeling reliant on the perpetrator or a person who is abusing their power. If someone can access a full, calm, and rested brain, they can usually make sound decisions. If they experience any fear or anxiety and are separated from others, they will not be making a full, well-rounded decision, and people who want to hold power know this as well.

For example, power abusers become adept at putting separation between loved ones of who they are abusing and the person being abused, or those who would be of help, by making the abused afraid to contact their loved ones. This makes the person experiencing abuse feel alone and then dependent, reliant upon, or trusting of the abuser because in isolation, the abuser is the only person they have access to and feel they can now depend upon.

A more tangible example of this occurring in the workplace is a senior leader who creates a workplace environment that separates the executives from the rest of the employees with executive-only lounges or areas. It creates an "us-versus-them" atmosphere and isolates the leaders and the employees from one another. Employees may then be fearful that if they overstep and enter that environment, they will be shunned or punished. It can be abusive as an adult to feel like you can be punished for simply walking through the "wrong" door. Or maybe someone on the team is fearful of their job role being infringed upon, so they separate themselves and silo their work to prevent collaboration and unity, making the team less efficient and divided. In this scenario, the abuser is a bit more removed than the personal connection of a romantic relationship, but the culture of leadership has allowed for someone to feel as if their job is in question and that it must be protected at all costs. That culture of leadership is an abuse of cultural power.

You can now understand what fuels the need for some to have control and power over others. It's not always the result of an ill-intentioned desire to hurt others—it usually is the result of a lack of assistance or help, or a basic human need for compassion and empathy that wasn't met when a child or adult was in search of it. Knowing this information does not provide justification or allowances for harmful acts against other human beings or living things. Rather, knowing how trauma manifests inside of someone over the course of their lifetime may provide clarity for how someone gets to the point of desiring and potentially becoming addicted to power over someone else, with complete disregard for others' thoughts or feelings. In other words, without empathy. In every case of someone exerting power over another in an unhealthy way, or leaning into their shadow powers, empathy is ignored, avoided, and in some cases, completely disregarded.

But how does a person get to the point where they are giving their power away willingly?

CHAPTER 5:

The Ins And Outs Of Fear: Power Given Away

Whatever the cause, we are all surrounded by people who are hurting or suffering in some way, and as a result, abusing power (or relying on shadow powers to get through life). In order to feel in control of their lives, they may use tactics to stay in a position of power, and as a result, control others as well. This usually ends up manifesting in using fear to control others and finding those who are willing to give their power away.

Power can also be given away sometimes without even realizing it is happening. Let's look further into this in the following example.

At work, your senior leadership team has always communicated well and acted in the best interest of employees. They may have great inclusive health care benefits, incredible performance incentives, and amazing employee perks. They communicate often about how well employees are doing and even publicly acknowledge employees by name in company-wide events and meetings. Your boss is by far one of your favorite and most trusted people in the business. Even though your boss has only been there for a little under a year, he has always given you autonomy and acknowledged your contribution to the team. He was a bit evasive once when you asked about a specific program you were interested in, but there was time to lean into that conversation, and it didn't cause you great concern. The majority of the relationships were positive and great for a successful team!

One day, your boss comes into a meeting and his tone changes. He says, "I can't tell you exactly what is going on, but it isn't great, and part of it is related to your performance on this last project." You immediately feel fear and get defensive. Because you trust and respect your boss, you couldn't possibly imagine letting him or this company down. You are shocked, but you trust your boss, so you start by asking questions. You want to know what happened. What was said? What should you do? All of which go mostly unanswered by him, or he gives vague answers. You tell him that you'll do anything necessary to fix any potential mistakes or harm you caused. He then asks you to put together a project plan that could solve what was wrong and to deliver that to him in two weeks. You get to work on that plan right after getting out of the meeting with your boss.

Two weeks later, you meet with your boss again and deliver the best work you have ever done in your life, and you are right! Your boss raves about your dedication and productivity and praises you for how quickly you were able to pull this solution together for your team and the business. You leave the meeting feeling a sense of accomplishment and take a deep breath of relief. After a few more weeks, there is a department-wide meeting. Your boss, and his boss—a member of the senior leadership team—are present, and you see that the name of your project plan is listed on the agenda as an item of discussion. You are feeling nervous, excited, and confused because your boss didn't even tell you that this project would be presented to the entire department today. Is he going to put you on the spot? Were you supposed to prepare for this?

You look at your boss, and he looks back at you with a smile and a thumbs up, which eases some of your anxiety, but you are still somewhat confused. After a while, the senior leader says, "And now on to the big news of the day," and you notice that the next agenda item is your project. He goes on to announce that your boss has been the brainchild of an amazing solution that is going to propel the business and allow the potential to bring in millions of savings, therefore dramatically increasing revenue over the second half of the fiscal year. Then he tells everyone that your boss is being promoted as a result and will be shifting to a new role in a different part of the business. Your name is never mentioned in association with the project.

In the scenario above, can you identify the point at which fear was used to manipulate your actions? At what point did you realize that you may have been controlled? Did you feel as though your power was taken from you? Journal your thoughts.

Events like this happen every day in businesses, schools, communities, and even families across the world. Fear and emotional manipulation go hand in hand. Fear is effective in maintaining control over others because it can paralyze and cause them to make decisions that they would not normally make. Fear turns on the amygdala, which turns *off* the decision-making part of the brain as we discussed in the previous chapters. Fear and isolation can cause anyone to be susceptible to manipulation when this happens.

Let us transfer this use of fear to our current American society. Every single day, we turn on the TV or unlock our smartphones and look at social media posts containing repeated negative images of news over and over and over again. We hear about bombings and earthquakes that kill hundreds or thousands of people. We hear about murder, hate crimes against people, shootings, war, and violence. For months, we've received constant messages that our government is shutting down access or support for whole groups of people that may be disenfranchised or historically marginalized. We have heard of funds being eliminated or diverted to places they have never been before, which also increases anxiety. Many of us don't know what news to trust or not, but we can all agree that the majority of what is reported is tragic and hard to hear.

Spreading fear as a mechanism of maintaining power has been widely used across historical contexts and even current political landscapes. We can observe the use of fear in election cycles, like in 2024, when 64 countries were engaged in critical election seasons, including China, England, Canada, Germany, France, Spain, India, the United States, and more. And once again, let me repeat that fear was not used only by one political party or another. Fear was used by all sides to persuade the other side. "He's gonna do this if…" or "She's gonna do this if…" or "We're gonna lose everything we hold dear if you don't vote for me." And when the conversations turned to facts, the facts were manipulated, skewed, or changed, and then the conversation shifted right back to, "But if you don't, then we are doomed."

When we use these tactics to keep people in a permanent state of fear, receivers can no longer make sound decisions because their brains handle this information as a constant threat. Recall the conversation about the brain shutting down the ability to think clearly when feeling fear or anxiety. When we are constantly bombarded with these threats of fear, how can we even find an opportunity to disconnect and let our brains return to a relaxed state in order to determine if the information is correct or not?

Through all of this, we may be tempted to point fingers at one political side being more manipulative than the other. We may want to say that one is absolutely wrong, while the other is absolutely right. But is that true? Or have we been manipulated to think a certain way rather than seeing more than one viewpoint at a time? Ultimately, what is the result of being forced to connect an opinion to a choice of right or wrong? This side or that side? Division. Division. Division.

The next question in my mind while doing this research was centered on the people who were being controlled, or, in other words, who gave their power away. I wondered, how could one person, let alone a whole population of people, allow someone to assume abuse of power over them, and in some cases even support it? Then, in turn, how can whole communities, cities, and nations also allow the same? Admittedly, this is a heavy question, and the answer contains more scientific explanations around fear and emotional manipulation.

When We Willingly Give Power Away

The thought of willingly giving your power away to someone else seems absurd and even laughable. I hate to be the bearer of bad news, but we all have experienced a loss of power over some aspects of our lives at some point.

Sometimes, power given away is a result of the stage of life you are in, and sometimes it's not always bad. When I was seven years old, I got a Huffy pink and purple sweet style bicycle for my birthday. It had pink handlebars with streamers, a detachable purple and pink fanny pack that hung in between the handlebars in the middle (it snapped around the handlebars), and purple glitter spokes on the wheels. It was very cute, and I felt very cool just riding on it. I had a friend who lived on the corner at the end of our street, and I would park my bike right on the corner of the sidewalk because her driveway was behind a fence, and that was too difficult to maneuver. I wanted people to see this bike! One day, my dad was driving home from work and saw the bike on the corner, and when I got home, he said something to me about how my bike could get stolen if I left it unattended on the corner. I thought nothing would happen to it, of course. So, I did it again, and he saw it again. When I got home, he yielded some parental power and said, "You better stop leaving that bike on the corner or someone is gonna steal it." I said, "Okay, Daddy!" My mom was carefully observing the conversation, but didn't say anything.

So, the next few times I went to my friend's house, I didn't leave it there. But then, I got comfortable again and left it right on the corner. This time, when I walked out of the backyard of my friend's house, it was gone. I panicked. I ran all around that house, down the street, and the side streets that all were dead ends. At this point, I was hysterically crying for three reasons. One, my bike was gone, and I loved it; two, I was scared that someone had taken it; and three, I was terrified of what was going to happen when I got home and told my parents what happened.

When I got home, my mom saw my face and I burst into tears. "Mommy, someone took it. Someone took my bike!" I was sobbing. Not too much time passed with her consoling me, while trying to tell me that my dad tried to tell me not to leave it there, and in walks my dad from the dining room into the kitchen. He saw my face and said, "What's wrong?" I barely got the words out, and then he replied, "Someone did take your bike then, huh?" I cried out, "Yessss," with heavy breaths.

Then, in his matter-of-fact tone, he said, "I took it. It's in the trunk. I got tired of telling you the same thing over and over again for you not to listen, so I put it in the trunk." And before I could react, I immediately saw my mom's facial expression turn from concern to anger. He didn't tell her either, and she was not happy about his teaching moment, and neither was I. I was still sobbing, and I said, "Daddy, you didn't have to do that. Why did you do that?" And my mom was silent. When my mom went silent, we all knew someone had done something wrong. I did not leave my bike on the corner ever again, so his plan worked, but my mom was not as forgiving for a few days.

That is an example of how I gave power away to my father, which he used as a source of manipulation, but in a way that was for my greater good. His motivation was protection and teaching me a lesson about safety and care of things that are important to me, as well as to be mindful of the potential for accidents and to prepare in advance. Some may say it was traumatic because I'm writing about it in a book (cue my laughter), but it wasn't harmful. It taught me a valuable life lesson—to take good care of your precious material items that are important to you. I let my father influence me, and his lesson stuck with me and affected my actions from that moment forward.

Think to yourself, when you were a five-year-old child (and if you lived in a healthy, non-abusive home), did you have control and power over your bedtime? Did you have power or control over where you went to school? Did you have power or control over your parents? Did you obey their (good-natured) instruction and discipline? It is likely that the answer to all of those questions is no, because at that stage of life, your parents did exert a level of power over you, and you willingly gave your power away to them. What choice did you have? Hopefully, they used that power to teach you some needed lessons throughout your life and to serve the greater whole, and not for harm.

In most healthy cases, children who give their power away have an inherent trust in others because the purpose of the parent or guardian exerting power was to teach positive life lessons that would guide the child into being a responsible adult. The child benefits from giving their power away. However, in some cases, giving that power away did not manifest in healthy behaviors because some people, even parents, abuse trust and power.

As we move into adulthood, though, and become independent adults, we often still find ourselves in situations where we have given our power away. Giving our power away goes beyond following an employer's instructions, or wearing professional attire when you would rather be in sneakers and jeans, or compromising with a partner on a disagreement. It's when we ignore ourselves, overshoot our level of empathy, fail to recognize the power and confidence in our own identities and unique gifts that we contribute to society, lack courage in our ability to decide for ourselves, and allow someone else to dictate what we do, say, or even think. Sometimes this is because of internal anxieties or fears that develop over time. Consider a work-life example:

Alex is a veteran, which most consider to be honorable and positive, outside of work. But Alex fears that revealing his role in the military while he served could lead to misconceptions about his mental state or that he can't be trusted at work. Alex becomes afraid that he could even lose his job or not be promoted. He is anxious and fears that people may discredit his experience in the military as not relevant. So, he hides this part of himself from his coworkers and his boss. He has given away the power, pride, and self-confidence of being a military service member.

In this example, fear is not a motivator, yet it suppresses the power that Alex used to feel when he was in the military. He feels that his experience of serving in the military is now a deficit when entering the civilian workforce. At first, Alex's military service is honorable, and the pride he feels in being a servicemember for all of those years is stripped away when he enters civilian life. To secure a living for himself, he has to let go of some of the power he held in being a military serviceperson in order to get a job where he believes he is misunderstood and where his military service could become a hindrance. He has to give up the power that he has held and known for so long to someone else simply because of the fear that he has of a leader in the civilian world not being empathetic to his transition or the skills he possesses that carry over into the workforce. This happens as a result of fear.

We may not always understand or realize why or when we are giving our power away. Some may give their power away for as long as they've lived—hiding parts of themselves both small and large things, deferring to others' opinions, shrinking themselves, and staying out of the way. But why?

How the Power of Fear Leads To Giving Power Away

This leads me to return to the discussion of fear, which I believe is the root of both exerting power over others in an unhealthy way *and* giving our power away. Why is fear so effective in the manipulation of others? Merriam-Webster defines fear differently, based on whether or not it is being used as a verb or a noun, yet all of the definitions center around the following:

- ✦ an *unpleasant,* often strong emotion caused by anticipation
- ✦ or awareness of *danger*
- ✦ *anxious* concern
- ✦ a profound *reverence and awe,* especially toward God
- ✦ reason for *alarm*
- ✦ To be *afraid* of
- ✦ To be *apprehensive*

When reading these definitions, it is clear that the emotions that are expressed from fear are largely negative—feelings that are unpleasant, such as danger, anxiety, and apprehension, are not fun feelings to experience. Only one of these could be taken as a positive definition, which is to have "reverence and awe toward God," in other words, "the fear of God." For those who are spiritual or religious, fearing God is what often keeps someone faithful, continuing to make positive decisions, and doing what is right for themself and others. I want to stress that this context is only positive when the fear of God, religious beliefs, and loyalties are not used as a form of justification for doing harm to others.

More interesting than its definitions is the science of fear and how it affects the body and the brain. Instead of rehashing this explanation again, we will do an activity. The following exercise will help you understand this more:

 ## Activity: Fear in the Body and Brain

NOTE: Please do not do this exercise if you have experienced a fearful emotional

trauma that will be triggering to you or cause a relapse in any recovery process that you are a part of. The intent of this exercise is not to retraumatize, yet help provide a real-time reaction to provide an in-the-moment alignment with the science. If you are able to complete this exercise safely, please continue. If not, or if you have any reservations, please skip the next paragraph and continue to read about the physical and mental scientific reactions to the feeling of fear.

I want you to take a deep breath and think of a time in your life that you experienced fear. This should be the type of fear that altered your future actions or decisions after the event was over. Maybe it was a moment like when I thought my bike was stolen, or when your boss told you that if you came back one minute late from your break, you were fired, so you have never taken a full break since, or any other moment in your life that could have altered how you behaved moving forward. Maybe it was a week ago when you were walking home alone at night. As you think about that scenario, just ponder the following questions:

+ When you think back on that moment of fear, were you thinking clearly?
+ Did you weigh all of the options available to you, or did you simply do what was needed in that exact moment?
+ Did you look back on that event and wonder why you made the decision you made?
+ Did you think to yourself that you would have handled it differently?

If you cannot think of a time for yourself, you can read about one of my own experiences. When I was pregnant with my second son, I was told in the final month of pregnancy that my blood pressure was higher than normal and my amniotic fluid levels had dropped to a level that could endanger the life of my unborn son. I was later told that I had preeclampsia and that if my blood pressure did not stabilize quickly, both of our lives were at risk. It became even more real and scary when my water broke, and I went into labor two weeks early. I saw and felt my blood pressure rising as we raced to the hospital. Gratefully, once at the hospital, the nurses were able to stabilize my pressure. I had the help of fast-acting medical staff and a smooth delivery with minimal health concerns in the process, but it was terrifying in the beginning because my life and the life of my unborn son were in danger.

After delivery, I remember a very serious discussion about my son possibly needing to be in the neonatal ICU for a brief time because his liver needed more time, and he had jaundice (which causes yellowing of the skin and eyes when the liver is not fully functioning). I can very easily close my eyes and place myself back in that mental space of fear. It is a memory that I will never forget because it was traumatic and scary, even though the outcome was positive, and my son continues to live a healthy life. Thankfully, there were people around me at that moment who were not in a state of fear, because my brain had completely shut down.

When you think back on your moment of fear, were you thinking clearly? Did you weigh all of the options available to you, or did you take an action that made the most sense quickly? Later, can you look back on that event and wonder why you made the decision you did? Do you think to yourself that you would have handled it differently if you could go back in time? (Jot those notes down in your journal).

When someone is afraid or feels fear, the body reacts physically. People may feel their heart racing, sweat, have tensed up muscles, experience heightened senses, or become muted, freeze, or begin to look around for ways to get help, or run. Depending on the scenario, these are normal responses to fear. It is a part of our fight, flight, or freeze reaction. And here comes my pre-medicine, biology teaching experience shining through!

In the brain, the first signal of fear comes from an observation from one of our five senses. When the brain interprets an observation as fear, the signal goes directly to the amygdala (pronounced: uh-mig-duh-la). The amygdala is a very small gland in the back of your brain, and it has a very important role in processing emotions. The amygdala also links those emotions in the creation of memories, learning, and to your senses. The amygdala is shaped like an almond and is a part of a larger network of nerves and glands in the brain called the limbic system. These are the parts of your brain that detect danger and control fear.[31] For example, if you are stung by a bee, the amygdala remembers that and attaches that memory to fear or danger when you see another bee flying too closely to you, because it has now associated fear with bee stings to protect you from being stung again. The amygdala plays a role in how we develop anxiety, learn things unconsciously (like remembering how to tie your shoes without trying), experience addiction, and interpret communication. Anxiety, unconscious thoughts (like bias), and addiction are all mechanisms that lead to power abuse, fear, and power given away, so the amygdala is a critical part of our human behavior.

Once the amygdala is activated, it releases hormones (adrenaline and cortisol) that signal stress reactions in the body. This is what causes physical changes in the body when we feel fear, like increased heart rate, rapid breathing, heightened alertness, or sweating.

What is even more important to know is that the release of these hormones indicates to the brain to turn off all signals being sent to a different part of the brain called the prefrontal cortex. This area of the brain is essentially located just behind your forehead. This part of the brain is responsible for making executive decisions when thinking and problem-solving.[32] This is why when some people are scared, they might "freeze," becoming paralyzed for a period, not knowing what to do or where to go. This is also why others make quick, rash decisions in the moment that would not make sense when the brain is in a calmer state ("flight"). If someone is afraid and they remain in that state, they probably will make decisions that they wouldn't normally make, and usually these decisions are not logical. They might just give their power away unknowingly and unintentionally. In this way, fear is the method of manipulation. It keeps someone from chronically making logical decisions and is a mechanism of causing others to willingly give power away.

Power and Oppression

This entire discussion about power over others and power being given away helps us understand how whole populations of people have been manipulated and how systems of oppression have been formed across the world. When I use the word oppression, for some it may automatically lead others to think that it only pertains to people who are naturally melanated or identify with a certain sexual orientation. I am intentionally not using the word "race" because race is a social construct, not a scientific one. Race was developed to classify people in early America. Oppression is the unjust treatment and control of another person. It is not limited to one group but is often used towards specific groups of people. It is symptomatic of a cycle of abuse and trauma that the oppressor has not healed from in themselves. And rather than walk through that pain to find positive coping strategies, they look to exert control and power over others because it is familiar, comfortable and feeds their dopamine fix from the power they feel.

This is why I argue that the lack of balance between empathy and power is the root cause of slavery and caste systems across the world. The symptoms of those horrific systems like racism, genocide, sexism, homophobia, disregard for laws and government regulation that protect those who have less or are treated unfairly, gerrymandering, redlining, and more, are a result of using isolation, fear, control, and manipulation.

It may feel trivial to narrow down the cause of 400 years of emotional, physical, and mental abuse, coupled with the loss of over 60 million lives, which is what happened during the enslavement of Africans and African American people, to a lack of balancing empathy and power, but it really is that simple. Imagine if the people who came to America had empathy for others they did not know, and power was used to serve the whole rather than just for self-interest. Imagine if the person who suggested and led the enslavement and killing of Native Americans when they set foot on their native land was countered by a group of people who balanced their culture with Native American culture. Imagine if they suggested coexisting or exchanging ways of life with the Native Americans to make for a more sustainable nation, where ideas were exchanged rather than whole cultures eliminated and power exerted over others. Sometimes, all it takes is a little empathy to balance the power, or a little power to balance out the empathy. Both are required. But in balance.

I was scrolling through Instagram reels one day, and I came across a woman named Kimberly Latrice Jones. She originally posted a video on TikTok, but if you use Instagram, you know that most of the videos on TikTok or other social media sites eventually end up being shared to Instagram, Facebook, and other platforms.

In this video, she compared the economic and financial oppression (control) of African American people as a result of the system of slavery to how it still affects the fair and equal opportunity of African Americans or Black people to the present day. As you read the script of her video below, think to yourself about how a lack of empathy and the enforcement of power to exert control over others are in imbalance.

Here is the script of her video:

> If I right now wanted to play Monopoly with you, and for 400 rounds of playing Monopoly I didn't allow you to have any money, I didn't allow you to have anything on the board, I didn't allow for you to have anything. And then we played another 50 rounds of Monopoly and everything that you gained and you earned while you were playing those rounds of Monopoly was taken from you. That was Tulsa, that was Rosewood. Those are places where we built Black economic wealth, where we were self-sufficient, where we owned our stores, where we owned our property, and they burned them to the ground. So that's 450 years.
>
> So for 400 rounds of Monopoly you don't get to play [for yourself] at all. Not only do you not get to play [for yourself], you have to play on behalf of the person that you are playing against. You have to play and make money and earn wealth for them, and then you have to turn it over to them. So then, for 50 rounds (years), you finally get a little bit, and you're allowed to play, and every time that they don't like the way that you're playing or that you're catching up or that you're doing something to be self-sufficient, they burn your game. They burn your cards. They burn your monopoly money and then finally, at the release and the onset of that, they

allow you to play and say, "Okay, now catch up."

Now, at this point, the only way you're going to catch up in the game is if the person shares the wealth, correct? So then, when you attempt to make suggestions about sharing the wealth, the psychological warfare starts to say, "Oh, you're an equal opportunity hire." So if I play 400 rounds of Monopoly with you and I had to play and give you every dime that I made, and then for 50 years every time that I played, you didn't like what I did, and you take it from me. How can you ever win? How can you win?[33]

Reflection Questions

Grab your journal and reflect on your thoughts after reading that passage. What emotions were stirred up inside of you? Did you think of any events in your own life or in your own heritage that you feel are comparable?

If you are in a team, practice being vulnerable with one another and share some of the thoughts that you had about the passage.

This activity is meant to be one for building relationships in your team and with yourself by examining the emotions you felt.

CHAPTER 6:

Empathy Is Power's Accountability Partner

We have dissected the meaning of power and what it is, and separately, we have dissected empathy and what it is. We have seen examples of each in various scenarios in the previous chapters. What has not been resolved is how to solve for an overabundance or a lack of either at any given time. There is an acronym, K.I.S.S., which many of us probably learned in our early school years. It stands for Keep It Simple, Stupid. Perhaps not the best acronym for teachers to use, now that we know it isn't really great to unintentionally or intentionally call kids or adults stupid, but nonetheless, I am about to keep it simple for you:

Empathy is the accountability partner for power, and power is the accountability partner for empathy.

Pretty simple, right? Yet, this has not been clearly stated as an actual concept or solution for division in this world. Sometimes the answer is right in front of you, and you just don't see it until someone points it out.

When I was an Assistant Principal, we were doing some important work on building culture in our school district, and we hired a man named Tim Kight to speak at our opening day staff meeting. Tim, whom I was fortunate to meet and receive training from several times, was the owner of Focus 3, a consulting group.[34] He was also the person who worked very closely with Urban Meyer when he was the head coach of the Ohio State University football team at the time. Urban Meyer wrote a book about their experience in shifting the team culture in a positive direction with Tim's help, *Above the Line*. Their work was credible based on the success of the Ohio State Football program during Urban Meyer's tenure as head coach. Tim taught me that sometimes you need someone to show you what you can't see, or an accountability partner.

During Tim's speeches (and any YouTube videos you find of Tim's talks), he loved to tell stories. I still tell a few of his stories he used as examples for us that day. The Dead Bush story is one.

He said, "One of my friends has a really nice house. The front lawn is well kept, the garden is neat and tidy, and he has two planters on either side of their front porch. Every day, because I've seen it, he walks out of the front door to go to his car to leave for work in the morning, and every day he returns through the front door. Sometimes multiple times a day. There were other times we would talk, and he would tell me about mowing, or tending to the landscaping, or something related to the yard.

As we got to know each other, eventually he invited my wife and I to his house, and we were very excited to get to know him and his wife better. When I pulled up in front of the house, it was just as he said. The lawn was gorgeous, and the landscaping was immaculate. I mean, I was a little bit jealous. So, my wife grabbed our thank you gift from the back seat, which was always a nice bottle of wine (or two), and we walk to the front door.

Well, just then, I glanced to my left and right and saw those two planters with the little baby evergreens planted inside, and they were as dead as a doornail. They were brown, the needles were falling off, and I remembered thinking to myself, *Now, what is happening here?* Just then, the door opened, and we walked in, and I didn't dare bring it up to my friend. Many days later, he and I were chatting, and I finally had the courage to ask him.

I said, 'Hey man, what's up with those two planters on your porch?'

He looked at me like he was confused and said, 'What are you talking about?'

And I said, 'Dude, are you serious? Those two bushes next to the front door.'

He replied, 'Oh yeah, the evergreens. What about them?'

And I said, 'Hey, man. They're dead. They aren't evergreen anymore; they are everbrown!' And he was baffled! Sure enough, he went home and looked at them, and he called me, and he said, 'I walk in and out of this house, and have been for months and months, and I have never noticed these bushes were dead.'

Tim ended his story by saying, "Sometimes, we get comfortable, and we don't see that things around us are changing. That's why you need an accountability partner."

Tim doesn't know it, but I shared that story in my final interview when I got my first corporate leadership position fresh out of high school administration. I told the story in the context of needing someone from outside the organization to point out their "dead bushes" and reveal what they don't see because they have been in the workplace environment too long to notice.

My former boss used to tell me, "I still think about those damn bushes," which we always laugh about. As I said, sometimes the answer is right in front of you, and you just don't see it.

It sounds simple, but in reality, it is not easy to do. Doing the work and learning how to see things about you that need work, but you may not realize are there, means you must have accountability partners. An accountability partner sees things you don't, and then they can point those things out to you. In the context of this book, it would be someone who can point out when your empathy and/or power are out of balance, and you may be the accountability partner to someone else, helping to balance their empathy and power.

First, balancing empathy and power requires some knowledge of how they interact with one another. Let's take the learning a click deeper and investigate the relationships between the two now.

I see power and empathy as on a continuum, like a sliding scale, volume control, or sound controls on a producer's sound board. We must find the right balance on the scale—or the perfect combination of sound controls on a sound board that produces an amazing song. We are all different, and so the degrees to which you move on the continuum are dependent on your own unique characteristics, just like different songs appeal to us in different ways.

The Power Continuum

POWER INFANT   POWER ADULT   POWER TYRANT

Power Infant

The Power Infant is just beginning to experience what it means to have some level of power in their own lives. Examples of this level of power would be an adult who has moved out of their parents' home, is living on their own for the first time, and is responsible for their own bills and expenses. Or maybe a power infant is a person who has just assumed their first position as a leader in some capacity after being an entry-level employee for years. This could be someone who takes on a team lead role or a supervisor position. They are new to the feeling and learning how to interact with power. The Power Infant is a person who still needs encouragement and support to feel like they can step into their own power and be confident. Because they are new to this idea of having "power," it takes time, training, and experience for the Power Infant to reach the next stage. The person at this stage, without the right level of support and training, is susceptible to giving away the power that they do have.

Think of someone you know (or maybe it is you) who got their first position of leadership, and you noticed how they struggled to come into their own. Maybe they second-guessed some of their decisions, but sometimes realized how they could make a difference. They began to have an influence on the people around them and learn more about what it means to be a leader. They still made mistakes and needed lots of advice, but slowly found their footing. Or, maybe suddenly, your former colleague at work, who was recently promoted to leadership for the first time, knew very little about executing in leadership. As they learned and grew more into their power and confidence, they began to drift a little further away from their original peer group, but continue to elevate and uplift those around them, including you! Eventually, they may begin rubbing elbows with mid-level management and influencing decisions that go a little bit further up the leadership pipeline. They may still struggle with thinking of themselves as a leader and look up to others for guidance regularly. A Power Infant is someone new to experiencing what power feels like for themselves and how it can influence others.

Power Adult

The Power Adult is mid-level power. Think of that same person who has now grown from entry-level leader to mid-level management and is now having lunches and happy hour with the senior leadership team, but still supports the entry-level staff in the way that they did before. They have updated their workplace colleague circle and now engage in networking events and are self-branding a bit in order to showcase their talents and experience to the level above them. In the workplace, this person has spent maybe five years in a senior-level position or on the higher end of the continuum in this area. They could be moving towards the C-suite, but they have not been in that position for an extended period of time yet. As my friend would say, "They start to smell themselves a little bit." They are confident in their decision-making skills, and no longer reach out to everyone for advice before making a move. Being a Power Adult is the goal because this amount of power is required to protect boundaries for mental health or to show evidence of strengths and abilities for success. At the same time, the Power Adult is still in touch with those who need help and has not forgotten how to reach back to the Power Infants to support them when needed.

At the entry to the middle level of this part of the continuum, when someone is a Power Adult, they still remember what it was like to just enter leadership. They hold their power but use it to serve the whole, not always the self. They are aware of their shadow powers and keep them in check. However, on the far right side of the Power Adult continuum, heading towards the next layer of power, a person might become more and more consumed with ego and self, and less with what is happening with people around them. They might be slipping into shadow powers as their authority and responsibilities increase.

This is a critical stage because if not balanced well with empathy, this stage can quickly drift into the next one, which shifts the power dynamic quite a bit. However, if they do start to lean in one way or the other, the Power Adult can be guided back towards the truth, just like a middle school student who may be influenced in a positive or negative way, but still has the opportunity to be guided to a balanced place. If they reach a point where the advice they receive or their accountability partner reinforces behaviors that benefit only the self, they might get to a point where the abuse of power is right on the cusp of their actions. This is steering them further from a balance of empathy and power. If a person is in this stage is on the borderline of entering a power addiction, or if you start to notice self-serving behaviors more often than those that serve the whole, this is the best time to intervene before it's too late.

Power Tyrant

Typically, when a person is abusing power or is using power for their own benefit, they are not concerned with thinking of others, and frankly, they don't want to. Power, as you now know is extremely addictive. The power abuser is what I refer to as the Power Tyrant—the furthest end of the continuum of power. When people already have a predisposition to addiction, the drug of choice sometimes doesn't matter. It can be much worse when that drug isn't illegal to use in high quantities, like sugar. The addiction to power is a drug of choice for some.

Addiction to power, like illegal substances, can also cause people to harm others intentionally just to remain in power, or make irrational decisions, spend money with the thought of earning more and more over time, and, in some cases, even commit crimes to maintain that power. It is the basis of greed. Addiction to this power is also a symptom of traumas that have not been healed, which I discussed in the previous chapter. It is of no surprise then that Power Tyrants are addicts of a legal drug, which is what makes it exceptionally difficult to help them be willing to acknowledge the addiction, what is causing it or realize that their levels of empathy and power are extremely imbalanced.

Power Tyrants also make rationalizations or justifications for why empathy for some and not others is justified. Maintaining connections with and supporting those who are wealthy or influential, for example, is completely acceptable to a Power Tyrant, but having empathy for someone who is in need or "less than" or will not contribute to maintaining their power or rise to higher levels of power is a waste of time to the Power Tyrant.

The deeper the Power Tyrant falls into their power addiction, abuse, and the (assumed) benefits of that power, the more difficult it becomes to turn them back around. Known more from the movie *Spiderman*, but modified from other historical eras, you may have heard that "with power comes great responsibility." For power tyrants, with great power comes great popularity, fame, and fortune, and those qualities attract others, which makes the Power Tyrant believe over time that what they are doing is positively impacting their lives and others'. People in this position may say things like, "Yes, I'm rich, but I worked hard to get here and everyone else can, too," or "I am doing great things for people every day. I just gave some money to a charity yesterday and I didn't have to do that. I could have kept the money," or "Everyone can work hard to get here just like I did so everyone can be treated the same. No special treatment is required."

The Power Tyrant has lost sight of, or maybe never had sight of, those who work hard with the same credentials and do not ever "get there." They might conveniently forget the advantages they received along the way. An increase in empathy for others is the antidote to this scenario, but the Power Tyrant is not interested in the very thing they need to become a more balanced leader for others.

The Empathy Continuum

Just as there is a continuum for power, there is a continuum for empathy. Power is the accountability partner to empathy when empathy grows to a level that causes harm rather than good. People who are empathetic by nature tend to lean into being even more empathetic rather than the opposite. Some people may say that those who are empathetic tend to be more emotional, and I would agree. However, not in the negative way that it may be intended. The way that it may be intended is to imply that empathetic people cry all of the time, think they know how others are thinking and feeling when they don't, or mimic other people's emotions. There is also a perception that showing any emotion at all implies weakness. Instead, being more empathetic means tapping into your emotions, and being aware of them. It is a sign of inner strength, and using that in balance with physical strength and skill is a combination that garners respect even in defeat.

The Empathy Continuum

COURTEOUS BYSTANDER   ACTIVE EMPATH   SILENT SUFFERER

Courteous Bystander

A person with entry-level empathy is what I call a Courteous Bystander. A courteous bystander is someone with a basic or very minimal amount of empathy and has a very difficult time with perspective-taking. They may have a basic awareness of others and can acknowledge the thoughts and feelings of others when it is overt and unavoidable, but will not go out of their way to extend themselves to help or listen to someone else. They are not rude, and they may be understanding at times, but usually only to people with whom they already have a favorable relationship. Going past the point of basic understanding begins to make them uncomfortable. This could also be confused with introversion on the surface, but it is different. An introvert may feel uncomfortable approaching someone to console them if they do not know the person very well, but they would still be able to express empathy towards others with those they trust if they are an empathetic person.

Typically, there is a reason why the courteous bystander gets uncomfortable—whether it is because they guard their own thoughts and feelings and do not want to be vulnerable, or they may feel like it is too invasive or not their business to get over involved in someone else's life. It is important to note, however, that Courteous Bystanders are not rude, yet they can sometimes give off the impression that they do not care for others. When faced with a difficult situation, the Courteous Bystander may listen and then walk over to a friend who is not involved, take a deep sigh of relief, and say, "Oh, thank God. I'm not equipped to handle or process that!" Or "Whew! I hope they can figure it out!" or "I sure hope they find some help, but I can't do it!" They will not say it to the person's face, but their body language might give off that vibe. They do not mean to be harmful but are so out of touch with their own emotions that trying to tap into someone else's feels overwhelming.

Those who are not empathetic, don't know how to be, or are uninterested in being empathetic towards others can be self-centered individuals. They have a difficult time sustaining healthy, positive long-term relationships because of their inability to see things from others' perspectives, which pushes others away. This may also be a defense mechanism of protection due to their own personal traumas or life experiences.

Active Empath

Over time, and with life experiences (or sometimes with help and encouragement), someone may learn how to become more empathetic towards others and reach this level of empathy. Sometimes, a person may just be naturally empathetic. This person is an Active Empath. Active Empaths are typically openly compassionate. When they see someone crying, it is difficult for them to ignore or walk away without checking to make sure that person is okay. They tap into personal experiences and use them to connect with others going through something similar in order to provide the right support.

Picture yourself leading a team of employees at a job. One of your employees comes to work and is not acting like themselves. You can tell from their mood and body language that they seem a little sad and distant. They aren't smiling like they usually do; they make mistakes they don't normally make, and it begins to worry you because you remember when you felt that way after your aunt passed away. You walk over to them and say, "Hey, is everything alright? You seem a little different today." The person reveals that their grandmother passed away the evening before, but they knew they couldn't call off work that soon. You may tear up as they share the news, and very calmly say, "I can imagine how hard this is. We have it covered today. Go home and take some time for yourself. Call me and let me know when you think you can return to work, and we can talk through that together." That is how an Active Empath might respond.

The goal for balancing empathy with power is to grow to *this* level of active empathy.

By creating the space to feel for others, you allow your emotional intelligence to shine in moments when intuition and feeling with others is warranted, yet you still have enough internal power to self-regulate and not become over-involved. Self-regulation is an important skill for people who are empathetic (or have learned how to be) and is based on knowing your own emotional boundaries. If people do not create boundaries for themselves and protect their own emotions, it can lead to the next stage of the continuum. This might look like: knowing your limits in what you can give to others, controlling your schedule so you have time to rest and reenergize, or not getting over-involved in others' problems, unless necessary. In contrast, someone who creates too many barriers will lean back to the left side of the continuum, which can make a person more disconnected. The key is learning what boundaries you need to put into place to protect yourself while showing empathy for others.

As a leader and certified emotional intelligence trainer, there are two books that I recommend if you want to learn how to become more emotionally intelligent, increase your own ability to self-regulate, and learn how to recognize and set boundaries in a healthy way. *The Four Agreements* by Don Miguel Ruiz details four "rules" we all should learn to develop, which help readers make better decisions for themselves. The book also teaches how to break free from the smaller "agreements" we have learned from various life experiences, which may inhibit our ability to be emotionally intelligent and connect with others and ourselves.[35] The other book, *Set Boundaries, Find Peace* by Nedra Glover Tawwab, was written by a licensed counselor and shares strategies to help achieve balance and illustrate what healthy boundaries are and mean for individuals. Tawwab's techniques are rooted in the latest research and best practices in cognitive behavioral therapy and unravel the root problems behind codependency, power struggles, anxiety, depression, burnout, and more.[36]

I have read each of these books myself (several times in fact). Everyone that I have recommended the books to, and who did the work suggested in the book, has raved about the positive changes they have experienced by putting that advice into practice for themselves and others. If you are a leader of a team or involved in an entire organization or school, and you have gotten to this point in the book thinking that your team still has more basic work to complete regarding empathy and boundaries, these two books are excellent ways to move towards emotional intelligence and active empathy.

I want to reiterate that this work could be a longer road for some than for others. In the words of Sheryl Crow, "No one said it would be easy, but no one said it'd be this hard. No one said it would be easy. But no one thought we'd come this far." The work will be worth it and make the journey towards balancing empathy and power much easier.

Silent Sufferer

A silent sufferer is overly empathetic. This person finds it difficult to even function when they see someone else going through a hard time, or they are overly joyful when someone they know (maybe even just slightly) is experiencing a happy moment. Ultimately, their emotions rest in the way the others around them feel at any given time.

The reason I have coined "Silent Sufferer" for an overly empathetic person is that their emotions are so easily influenced by others that they are never internally regulated or balanced, and suffer emotionally as a result.

Silent Sufferers are on an emotional roller coaster (cue the song by Vivian Green). There is no regularity or balanced mental health. They may be easily manipulated, or even worse, abused by others or themselves, because their sense of self rests in the emotions and beliefs of others. Silent Sufferers are excessive people pleasers, often caring more about what others think about them than they do about themselves. At its height, a Silent Sufferer is deep in codependency. It is a very hard life to live, and like the Power Tyrant on the extreme end of the power continuum, it is very difficult to pull the Silent Sufferer back towards the middle. A Silent Sufferer will have to confront their innate desire to serve others before themselves and learn that their wants and desires are important. They might have to learn how to discover what *they* want without others influencing their decisions, concerns, and actions. Learning how to set healthy boundaries for their own realization of power, balanced with empathy, is important for the Silent Sufferer.

The Goal: Power Adult / Active Empath

Now that we see the continuums of empathy and power, let's look at them side by side below:

Power Adult/Active Empath

POWER INFANT	POWER ADULT	POWER TYRANT
COURTEOUS BYSTANDER	ACTIVE EMPATH	SILENT SUFFERER

At the start of this chapter, I stated how simple it was to think that power is the accountability partner to empathy and vice versa. Essentially, the idea is moving from the extreme end of the continuum towards the middle for balance—to become an Active Empath and Power Adult—someone who recognizes their "power," or their abilities and influence, while remaining properly empathetic towards and aware of others.

To paint the picture of the balanced Active Empath and Power Adult, I think of those who have positions of power and use that power to also be empathetic towards others. You may know someone like this in your own workplace, school, or organization. Usually, they are people's favorite leaders because, while they definitely hold a level of authority and stand firm in their decisions, they may take time to explain why those decisions were made or analyze how the decisions will affect the people across their teams. They provide support and solutions for those who are in need and provide more opportunities for those who are ready for a boost in responsibility. Like most other real-life scenarios involving human behavior and unpredictable situations, there may be events or times that call for more power and less empathy, or less power and more empathy. As you learn and practice, you will know when and how to adjust. The only way to do that is to remain dedicated to the person that balances serving the whole and the self equally, and to have trusted people in your life who can help maintain that balance.

Empathy and power are accountable to each other. In the absence of one, the scale will tip in the opposite direction. A comedian I heard once, Michelle Wolf, did a "bit" about women who "have it all." She replies that she does not want to have it all. She gave the example of going to a buffet and eating everything available in the buffet. Her words were, "Never have I left a buffet and felt great about myself for eating everything that I could in the hopes of eating the whole damn buffet!" As I said in earlier chapters, too much of anything is *too much*. Too much of anything for the body is usually not a good thing, even if it is something healthy, because it becomes excessive, obsessive, and sometimes even abusive. It is no different in the discussion about empathy and power and why finding the right balance is so important.

The next logical question is, how? How do you find that balance? What is the right balance for you? What if you notice someone slipping into an imbalance where intervention is needed? They are all questions that will be answered soon, but before I address those questions, it is first important to settle into the belief that more than one thing can be true at the same time.

The idea of power and empathy working in tandem with one another is only successful if a person is able to believe that two things can be true at once.

CHAPTER 7:

Two Things Can Be True

There is a time and place when it's necessary to make a choice between two things. Some examples of dichotomous decisions we face are whether to get married or not, to go to college or not (or which school to pick), to have children or not, choosing between two cars to purchase, and so many more! Some of the largest decisions in our lives might feel like we have to choose between two extremes.

However, there are decisions that are less black and white and are more gray, and typically those involve ethical and moral decisions where there could be more than one outcome or right answer for each individual scenario. In the context of learning how to balance empathy and power, dichotomies can become dangerous and divisive. The concepts discussed in this book are not meant to convince someone to be solely more empathetic or power-hungry. In order for the concepts, learning, and solutions in this book to work for you and others, you must believe that two things can coexist at the same time, and honestly believe that there could always be a best, third option as you work to restore balance. I have a close friend to thank for saying this to me almost daily.

This is the foundation of believing that a person can have power and be empathetic all at the same time. The dynamics between how empathy and power present themselves in your life may ebb and flow in different directions at any given time (like the ocean), but they all exist together in harmony.

You can also think of dichotomies as *polarities*, or two concepts that are on opposite sides, like the north and south poles of the Earth. Brian Emerson and Kelly Lewis are two professional leadership coaches who co-wrote the book, *Navigating Polarities: Using Both/And Thinking to Lead Transformation* in 2019.[37] In this excellent book, they use research from Barry Johnson, who introduced polarity theory.[38]

The polarity theory is the idea that a problem can be solved, or an impasse can be surpassed, while using two polar opposite viewpoints at the same time. He describes polarities as "pairs that can work together to manage problems interdependently rather than as opposing views." Polarities, according to Johnson, are the opposing options that different people generate to solve a singular problem. His theory is that by seeing, mapping, assessing, learning, and leveraging the differences, a best third option can be considered so that all viewpoints are utilized in the solution. *Navigating Polarities* introduces and explains this concept and offers a framework solution to work through problems in the workplace, teams, or other scenarios where two polar opposite solutions are introduced, and teams may have come to an impasse.

This impasse is usually due to *either/or thinking*, such as, "either I hire person A or I hire person B," or "either I eat meat or I'm a vegetarian." The authors suggest that either/or thinking is a way of problem solving that requires one or two right answers, which are usually exclusive of one another.

Often, however, we face a problem that requires a solution, but there are a variety of solutions that could solve the problem. It isn't easy as a "this" or "that." In other words, there is more than one or two solutions, and there could even potentially be an infinite number of solutions. In our daily lives, at work, at school, and inside teams or in personal relationships, it becomes evident that a group of people may have several different solutions to the same problem, most of which are opposite to one another.

On top of that, when people feel very confident that their solution is "right" and that the other person's solution is "wrong," it can lead to conflict, arguments, delays in production or work output, or, in extreme cases, the dismantling of an organization. Emerson and Lewis counter polarities with the idea of *both/and thinking* and encourage readers to see that two (or more) things can be true at once—this belief is essential to the success of any team that is addressing a problem.

Both/And When Balancing Empathy and Power

Balancing empathy and power is needed in multiple industries, personal relationships, and the relationship with oneself. To find the balance, both-and/thinking is required. It will be hard—almost impossible—to balance empathy and power if we believe we must choose *either* one *or* the other. To heal division, we must believe that *both/and* thinking is possible and obtainable in more situations than not. When we think of decisions as either/or in every single scenario, it automatically reinforces a divisive process and outcome because, inherently, that means someone must choose one or the other. Both/and thinking means that we consider all sides, all options in a scenario, and collectively, collaboratively produce a solution that benefits the whole while keeping all opinions in mind.

We must believe that even if someone else introduces a possible solution that is different than ours, it does not make our solution wrong and theirs right. We must know when to own our beliefs and strengths, and when to put ourselves in others' shoes. We must know that while we have had our experiences, others' experiences might counter ours. This doesn't make someone right or wrong; it just makes it different. A person can love both red and white wine. A person in the workplace can enjoy being a tax consultant and also have skills as a human resources leader. It doesn't make them wrong; it makes them different and multidimensional and gives them the ability to showcase those various skills. Both can be true.

In the same way, we must feel *both* confident in our power *and* empathetic towards others. By allowing ourselves to consider other options, we actively work towards a balance of empathy and power, rather than resisting and leaning further into one side of the continuum. To balance, we must open our minds up to consider the opinion of others and the root of that opinion. Does what they say have validity? Is there something from their perspective that can be helpful? These considerations are important in using both empathy and power as we go about our day-to-day lives. Whether it's at work, in conversations with loved ones, in decision-making, or for a Fortune 500 company, this balance enhances innovation, unleashes creativity, empowers others, and increases the engagement and ownership of the work for the people who work hard to achieve business or relationship goals.

Power Adult/Active Empath

POWER INFANT	POWER ADULT	POWER TYRANT

COURTEOUS BYSTANDER	ACTIVE EMPATH	SILENT SUFFERER

Examine again the continuum diagram of empathy and power again from the previous chapter. You can see two polarities: either someone can be a Silent Sufferer (extreme empath), or someone can be a Power Tyrant (extreme power). Someone could be a Courteous Bystander or a Power Infant. But does that mean there is no middle ground to be found or developed? Absolutely not!

How, then, do people navigate towards a solution when there are two polarities or with more than two people, while considering all ideas and opinions as a part of the potential solution? Well, one way is to read the book *Navigating Polarities*, where a full framework and resources, in addition to the summary I provided above, can help walk readers through how to get to the best third option in order to prevent divisive *either/or* decisions. If that is not an option for you based on time or budget, there is another way to lead a group of opposing, divisive sides to a decision that promotes unity and inclusion of all perspectives. The largest part of the work is being willing to listen and open to accepting that our way of thinking is not the only way. Outside of this researched option above, you can read below for another activity that I have participated in and led for others: Home Group Task Group.

Home Group, Task Group

The Home Group, Task Group concept is really helpful when developing the belief that two things can be true at once. To describe this, here is a short story about how it was used when it was introduced in my life. In the Summer of 2009, I decided to go back to school for a third time to get a master's degree in educational administration. Educational administration is very similar to business administration in many ways, except for one very large way: as an educational administrator, you do not just manage adults, like teachers, parents, and community members; you also manage children, adolescents, and teens. It is sometimes difficult for people to imagine what it is like to be an administrator at the elementary, middle, or high school level. We see ideas of what it may be like on television and in movies, but those characterizations of principals and assistant principals typically center on parent meetings or disciplining a child. It puts an image into our heads about what educational administrators do all day long, like the principal in *Ferris Bueller*, spending his entire day trying to catch him for skipping one day of school.

It was hard for me to imagine what it meant to be an educational administrator until I went through a summer intensive program with a group of about 30 teachers who were each seeking to become administrators. In this program, we worked together in groups often, and there were people with some very strong opinions about how to get things done.

Early on in the program, the professors separated us into five groups and informed us that we were going to work in these groups to design our final closing celebration, which was like the graduation for our time together in the summer. The only parameters that were given to us were the following: the cohort would be divided into several groups of five students in the class, there were only five total options for roles that each group member could have, which must be decided once in the group, and that group was called our "home group." We would be given a specific amount of time in our home group to share outcomes and make decisions. Once the roles were determined, we also had a specific amount of time in what was called our "task group." This group consisted of everyone who had the same role in their own home groups. So, if you were a note-taker X in your home group, you would meet up with the four other note-takers in your "task group" to share out ideas and come to a consensus. It was the job of the task group to discuss ideas and make decisions that we would then take back to our home group for discussion.

We were given the following additional guidance: if we found ourselves in disagreement with any group on how to move forward, we were to ask ourselves two questions: 1) Were my opinions and ideas considered in the final decision? and 2) if the decision is something I disagree with, can I live with it?

After they finished giving us the instructions, the professors closed their lecture with three words: "Trust the Process." At first, we had no idea what they were talking about. We all thought, "trust the process? Um, okay?" Quickly, we found out why they said that.

You can probably picture how awkward everyone was in the beginning. There were a few teachers from our cohort who knew each other because they were in the same school or in the same district, but many of us did not know each other before the program, and we had only spent six weeks together as a cohort. There were varying degrees of personalities in the cohort as a whole, and those personalities came into conflict in this activity. There were some people who were quiet, shy, or just went along with things because they wanted to avoid conflict. There were some who were very strongly opinionated, some who were short and impatient, some who were extroverted, and some who had strong opinions but, because they were introverted, would not speak up and held contempt in conversations. The groups were a journey, and several times we would get to a point where we just had to ask ourselves, "Can I live with this if this is the outcome?" I've heard others phrase this as, "Is this the battle I want to fight?" or "Is this a non-negotiable?" or "Is this the hill I want to die on?"

Every time we broke into home group/task group in class, the professors would send us to our groups saying, "Trust the process." The process did eventually work, and it became the mantra for our leadership cohort, and still is to this day, with many of the members of the cohort with whom I have remained in close contact. In fact, one of our cohort members went through a long journey to fight a life-threatening cancer, and he even said in a public post, "I'm trusting the process," and we all knew why he said that and what it meant. He is well and healthy today. We came to trust the process because we learned that while we had conflict, we were made to collaborate to find the best solution—one that wasn't just one opinion or the other, but fused together from multiple ideas into something that worked better in some cases.

The most important lesson we all learned during this planning process is that in the end, everyone's opinions were considered, no one's singular opinion was the final decision, and we all were a part of the outcome. When we let go and "trust the process," the planning got better and felt inclusive of all thoughts. There were no winners and losers. No one was right or wrong. Everyone had a role to play, and their opinion was considered and, in some cases, used. There was no either/or. There was no dichotomous thinking: we leaned into both/and decision-making.

When you think about how this relates to healing division with empathy and power in this process, we were all forced to find a way to be empathetic and to listen to others when it was their turn to share or talk. We also learned that to be heard sometimes, you have to stand in your own power and hold boundaries when necessary. This all made the celebration much more meaningful to all of us involved.

The connection between navigating polarities and the home group/task group is that when solving problems, thinking of others and using all opinions to create the best third or fourth option, rather than creating a dichotomous choice to solve a problem, is one of the best ways to balance empathy and power. These frameworks prove that both can coexist.

If you're leading a team or have a leadership position, consider using the framework for a home group/task group within your organization. If this isn't the right time to incorporate a task like this, consider finding other ways to incorporate navigating polarities into the culture of your team, organization, or school.

If you are having trouble thinking of ways to come to a unified solution, you can reach out to me for help and guidance with consulting or seek out local college professors that specialize in change and strategies for educational administrators. They have a multitude of resources at their fingertips, and they are always willing to partner with people in the workforce.

Fighting Division with Unified Decisions

In our world today, we are facing very complicated and divisive issues. In America, specifically, our country has become increasingly contentious as people navigate their daily lives with those around them. America has always had divisive issues among its people at any given time in history, which has led to actual war when communication did not work.

I would also argue that those in positions of power often use either/or thinking, instead of both/and thinking, which reinforces the idea that one side is right and the other is wrong, rather than exploring how two things can be true—or that empathy and power can coexist.

There has been a lack of government leaders who advocate for and work together to create solutions that are empathetic, hold personal power for themselves and those they represent, and still consider all opinions involved. That is, in fact, what democracy is intended for—to hear the voice of the people and consider all voices, but we seem to have lost it. The concept of "reaching across the aisle" is a distant and rare memory in today's times. Consider the governmental leaders you think of: how often is their narrative or rhetoric focused on their own agendas rather than finding commonalities with other politicians, or even other political parties with differing opinions and beliefs?

I believe that our country's current division is due to the imbalance of empathy and power. If we do not have people working to create solutions, using both/and thinking, and to balance empathy and power, rather than becoming power tyrants or silent sufferers, we will remain a divided people.

"Divide and conquer" was not a phrase developed out of a lack of evidence. If a Power Tyrant is successful in creating division, he can conquer others more easily, and the best way to do that is to remove educational opportunities for all. Access to and advocacy for advanced education widens perspectives and invites curiosity. Removing educational access closes global views, instills fear, and spreads either/or thinking. One creates division by narrowing the ability for perspective taking or empathy and kindness, and pits people against one another through isolation.

Most people know that there is a basic ground rule for soldiers: "No one goes into battle alone," or for those in dangerous jobs like firefighters and police officers, some have the same rule: "No one is allowed to be alone at any time while entering, operating in, or exiting a building."[39] Rarely, if ever, are people in these jobs to do anything alone, because when divided or acting alone, they are less likely to be safe and successful in their task or mission.

At this time in history, the term "diversity, equity, and inclusion" has been reduced to the acronym DEI. When DEI is discussed in the political arena, it is often vilified as work that favors certain people over others or as a discriminatory practice. Therefore, it's portrayed as a divisive concept— it's portrayed as some having power over others. DEI can even seem like an either/or concept because to some, it feels like "if it isn't us, then it's them" rather than understanding that two things can be true and everyone benefits. Interestingly, let's investigate the opposite meaning of these words. The opposite of diversity is *sameness* or one type of something, which, since Europeans invaded America, has never been the case for those who live in our country. The opposite of equity is *inequity*, or a lack of fairness. Finally, the opposite of inclusion is *exclusion*. A society that excludes people is one centered on division and power abuse—some people are in, some are out.

When we villainize concepts like diversity and inclusion, or minimize the importance of workplace culture and engagement, or focus more on money and products than people, eventually those businesses and workplace environments will fail to adapt to the changing global society around them. Further, we negate the efforts to create connections in our communities, stimulate unity, enhance innovation, and keep our country representative of what it is and always has been: a country of diverse people who all have a voice that contributes to the humanity of our nation.

A quote from one of my favorite movies, *School Daze* (1988), directed by Spike Lee, is "a people united will never be defeated."[40] How true. I encourage you to watch it after finishing this book and see how solutions can be applied based on the issues that surface in the film. Balancing empathy and power increases the connection among and between others, uniting us and making us all stronger. We may be vastly different from others in several ways, and allowing us to unify to create an environment that we can all be proud to be a part of is beneficial to our society.

 ## Activity: Either/Or or Both/And?

Let's work through any either/or thinking that may exist in you first, and then we'll practice how to replace it with both/and thinking instead. You can complete this individually or in a team. Grab your journal and pen or type into the notes section of your tablet or laptop, and answer the following questions:

Self-Discovery Into Your Own Either/Or Thinking:

+ What are the non-negotiables in your life? These could be what you are unwilling to compromise on, like religion, whether you would get married or not, or where you want to live.

+ What are the arguments that you have gotten into with someone where you were passionate about a subject and came to a complete impasse with another person?

+ Do you allow yourself to consider others' opinions when you are in disagreement with them? Or, do you always stick to your original thought and ignore others'? If yes, how? If no, why?

+ In these conversations, if you had trouble considering the other person's viewpoints, what was it about their opinion that made them so passionate about it? What was their reasoning? Did you ask?

+ Is it possible that there is a part of their opinion that may actually be understandable?

+ Do you find that more of these arguments or moments of impasse happen more at work, in school, or in personal relationships?

+ Do you believe that two things can be true at once? What are some examples of things in your life that are true, even if they seem contradictory? For example, maybe you love going to the beach and being in the mountains, or maybe you are a person who wants to be in a committed relationship and consider yourself religious, but you don't believe in the concept of marriage.

✦ How do you navigate listening to opposing points of view and considering how parts of those views could be beneficial?

✦ Choose a hot-button topic that you are passionate about. Maybe it is prison reform or free and mandatory preschool education for all, or that pineapple belongs on pizza (feel free to pick your own). Write down what side of the argument you agree with the most (example: you are pro-preschool education). Now, imagine you are preparing for a debate and have to argue the opposing side. Write it out and prepare for it. Are there facts or opinions from the opposite viewpoint you could actually agree or compromise on? Does this change anything for you?

Optional Team Exercise:

As I close this chapter, I encourage your team to think about an issue in the workplace that has your department or workforce split into two very opinionated factions. If you are an educator, perhaps half of the teachers or professors in your department think the instructional philosophy should be more personalized learning for the student, while the other half think it is best to return to a more traditional approach to instruction. If possible, try discussing your problem using the following structure:

✦ First, come to a consensus on what issue you want to discuss.

✦ Second, have everyone write down why they believe their approach to the issue is the best. What are the benefits of moving forward with their approach? (A tip: If you are all together in the same room, have people write separate thoughts on Post-Its and have them place the Post-Its on a wall. If you are in a virtual space, use a tool like a Miro Board or shared file for people to type their thoughts into the document.

✦ Third, group the thoughts into common categories and go through them, asking those who shared an opinion to explain it.

✦ Fourth, ask the group to pick one or two thoughts or ideas they agree with from the side that is in opposition to your own opinion.

✦ Finally, ask this question to the group: How can parts of each viewpoint be included in a final solution that allows for all voices to be considered in the final selection?

Record and synthesize with your leaders, and then share the results with your team.

CHAPTER 8:

B.L.U.E.Print Process -
Balancing Empathy & Power in Action

The Balance B.L.U.E.Print © is a framework that approaches problem solving in leadership and communities, particularly those due to an imbalance in power and empathy, using a multidimensional approach. This approach was developed using my personal leadership experience as well as research learned during my career and educational degrees. The key to this approach is to start by working on the self in an effort to change behaviors and patterns of thinking, so that they can then be recognized when working with others.

Every individual, group, team, community, or organization needs different solutions to their problems of imbalance because each problem or issue is unique to their circumstances. This framework provides the structure to work through those complex issues one step at a time. The goal is to address the larger root cause and provide a holistic, high-level view of the solution so that the right steps can be applied to any problem or issue.

The Balance B.L.U.E.Print © is not specific to any industry, sector, person, or group of people, and after introducing and explaining the solution, I will give examples of how the framework can be used differently in some of those sectors, such as in the private vs. public, or for-profit vs. non-profit. I have been a professional in many areas and industries, and can appreciate the need for showing how something can be practiced in different areas to deepen the understanding of the concept. We will get through the framework step-by-step. As you read, just think of me as your own personal coach.

By now, you should have a solid understanding of empathy and power, how they connect to one another, what happens when they are imbalanced, and how the imbalance affects all parts of our society, workplaces, and industries. I will continue to use the terminology you have learned in other chapters, including the following terms: navigating polarity, shadow power, the power landscape, the differences between empathy and sympathy, and more. Be sure that you are familiar with these terms, but also use the book as your own personal file folder. Grab some sticky notes or fold pages down so you can flag those pages and easily refer to them when needed.

The solution that follows will detail the steps in creating a plan, strategizing, and starting actionable steps to solve for the power versus empathy imbalance, regardless of where or in whom the imbalance is discovered. Keep in mind that I am not telling you exactly how to solve your specific problem. Recall my warning in the opening chapter that telling you what to do or giving you a script for what to say for the infinite number of unique issues in each environment is not possible. Yet, I am giving you the framework to work through the imbalance and create your own customized solution. For some, it is difficult to see the difference between a framework and a customized script, so here is an example.

When I was an assistant principal, I took on a "fixer" persona, as many administrators do, because a lot of the work in admin was managing thousands of kids and adults all day, every day, as well as community members. There is a lot of work involved in putting out little fires throughout the day. If a staff member gets sick in the middle of the school day and can't teach anymore, I would have to arrange coverage quickly and have the class monitored for the remainder of the day—problem solved. Or, if a district representative came to us and said, "We will not be sending half of the students home while one grade level takes a state exam. We can't disturb the other students, and we can only use two-thirds of the school. What are we going to do?" I had to figure that out, solve the problem, and tell him what we were doing. Or, if a teacher came to me and said, "I'm having trouble with a particular student, and I've tried all that I know to try. What am I doing wrong, or how can I move forward with this student?" I had to come up with optional solutions to coach that teacher. Those are specific problems with specific solutions, and I communicated the specific answer.

The difference between that and the framework I've developed is that I will give you the *tools* to understand your situation and approach it correctly, not the *answer*. In my work as a corporate executive, I have had several adults come to me and say, "I want to do the right thing, but I don't want to say something wrong. Can't you just tell me what to say?" My response was always, "There are an infinite number of scenarios and possibilities when dealing with human people. There is no possible way that I can give you all of the words to say. What you can do is adjust your approach, your mindset, and your response in relation to each scenario and do some of your own education." That is what these steps in the framework will provide for you: a way to adjust your approach, mindset, and behaviors, and have the steps to respond to an act accordingly.

In *Navigating Polarities*, the authors do not provide a specific answer for every problem, yet in doing the work of solving polarities, the framework and steps provided help guide readers to the solution that is best for that scenario. There are problems that have a fix and a specific answer, and there are problems with more than one solution, which require a framework so you can develop the solution right for you. Every time I discuss this, it reminds me of my dad.

My dad was phenomenal at solving problems (or so we thought). We always felt like he told us exactly what to do when we had an issue, and we came to him. "Daddy! What should I do?" was often a phrase that my sister and I echoed growing up. When he passed away, we thought, "Now, who is going to tell me what to do?"' And later I realized, he never told us what to do or fixed the problems for us. He listened, asked the right questions, and helped coach us to solve the problem ourselves, and we didn't even realize it. That is what the Balance B.L.U.E.Print © will accomplish for you.

B.L.U.E.

The color blue often represents a color of calm and peace. Blue just so happens to be my favorite color because when I think of blue, I think of the beautiful shades of blue water on the gorgeous island of Aruba; I think of a warm day with a beautiful blue sky, or even the calming blue light in a day spa. Ahhh... can't you just feel the calmness that blue creates? Interestingly, blue is often equated to the word "clear," as in clear blue skies or crystal-clear blue water. The design of the Balance B.L.U.E.Print © will make *clear* what needs to be addressed to correct the imbalance of empathy and power.

B.L.U.E. is also a mnemonic device, with each letter representing the steps in the solution framework. These are concrete action steps to follow that will guide you to a solution with a four-phased approach. The phases of the action plan are below:

B - Begin Within
L - Learn & Locate
U - Unify & Build
E - Enact & Nurture

Okay! Here we are at the start of the action steps. If you have been reading for a while, this is a great time for a brain break so that you come back refreshed and ready to digest the information. When you return, you will want the following:

✦ If you are a person who likes to write in a book, you will want to have a pen or a highlighter nearby, and if you are like me, you will also want small, sticky notes or small, sticky bookmarkers. I'm obsessed with sticky notes. You may also want your journal that you have been taking notes in throughout the book.

✦ If you use tech to process or store notes, you may still want to have a pen, highlighter, or small sticky notes to flag sections. If you used your device when you were journaling throughout the book, be sure to pull your notes up so that you can refer to them when needed.

When you are ready, imagine the calmest voice you can. After you read this, close your eyes and take a deep breath. Think of that calming voice telling you, "I can do this. One step at a time." Repeat that to yourself three times as you take three slow deep breaths. Then open your eyes and put on your game face! It's time to lock in and do work!

B.L.U.E. Phase One: Begin Within
Time: 2-3 Months or 1 Quarter

This is the introductory phase of the work, and the purpose is self-reflection and awareness. If you were doing the work as you read the book, then, lucky for you, much of this work has already been accomplished. In this phase, the work is internal. It is about examining your emotions, potential biases, and your own positionality before engaging with others. If you have not done this work as you were reading, go back into the earlier chapters and find the activity prompts and start working through those questions as a starting point. Yes, just a starting point, because there are so many other opportunities for investigating the self.

If you are acting alone, then this step will take as long as it takes for you to sort through it all and gather some insights and conclusions. If you are working as a team, then this step needs to be completed by each member of your team before moving forward. When preparing to do this work, carve out time in your plan for processing, which means after each step, you will need to think about the work you want to do and discuss it with your team. This also means sharing your personal learnings and information you've read throughout the book.

It is important to note that it isn't mandatory to share what you're learning with others, even if you're doing this work as a team. Allow the space for it, but for some people on the team, it may become deeply personal, and they may not be ready or willing to share, and that is okay. The important part is that they do the work. If you are uncertain about whether or not they have completed that work, the next step will be helpful.

After you do some self-reflection and journaling through prompts, you will want to dig a little deeper and get some research-based assistance. There are assessments you can purchase and some that are reputable and free. Assessments that are from magazines, social media, and unreputable websites that read more like fun quizzes and are not backed by research or a scientific philosophy will not help you. Using the right assessments on a team is also helpful because they provide a unified way of discussing insights without invading the privacy of others.

Some assessments that I have found to be reputable and helpful in this journey are listed below. Please note, this is not an exhaustive list, and I do not have any personal ties to these organizations, but they are the assessments that I hear of being used most commonly in multiple industries.

✦   Personality and Intelligence Assessments

  o No, I am not talking about the 10-question quizzes that you find on *Buzzfeed* or in a magazine that asks, "What Celebrity Matches My Personality?" Those are fun, but not helpful in this exercise. There are several reputable personality and intelligence assessments. Some measure ability, some measure intellectual intelligence, some measure emotional intelligence, and some measure identity. Some measure fixed traits, and some measure traits in a snapshot of time, yet suggest a growth mindset of potential.

  o I have taken the following assessments and found them to be helpful: Gallup StrengthsFinder, Myers-Briggs Type Indicator, Blue EQ, and Insights Discovery Profile

✦   A 360 Assessment

  o A 360 assessment is one that you take yourself and also asks you to identify members of your trusted circle, both at work and in your personal life. They answer the same questions that you answered about yourself, and then you receive results that help you to see if your perception of yourself aligns or matches with the perception that others have of you. It is vulnerable and it can be met with a bit of anxiety for some, but it proves to be very enlightening in finding your own areas of bias or blind spots.

o I have used the DiSC assessment, but there are several others that have been noted to be reputable, such as: Korn Ferry 360, The Leadership Circle Profile (LCP), and the Center for Creative Leadership (CCL).

✦ Anti-Bias Assessment

o An anti-bias assessment is one that can help identify areas of unconscious bias. Recall that these biases form from the areas of our brain that create patterns and group information into a category without us realizing it. Our formed bias is all based on our life experiences, so it doesn't make it wrong unless we do not do the work to uncover them or create new life experiences that uncover them. This is also a vulnerable journey and one that even members of the team who want to do the work may be resistant to or reluctant to complete. It is difficult work.

o I have used the HBDI or Herrmann Brain Dominance Instrument and Project Implicit Association Test (by Harvard University). The HBDI is somewhat of a combination test for personality, but measures dominant preferences, thereby also identifying areas of avoidance or other biases.

This step is also a great opportunity to utilize executive coaches, experts, books, online video resources like TED talks, and more to gather as much information about yourself as you can. A few of my favorite TED talks that provide perspective and cause you to think about your own thinking (reaching more of a metacognitive level) are:

+ Valarie Alexander: How to Outsmart Your Own Unconscious Bias
+ Chimamanda Ngozi Adichie: The Danger of a Single Story
+ Brene Brown: The Power of Vulnerability
+ Simon Sinek: How Great Leaders Inspire Action

After you have completed this step, sit down with yourself or your team and answer the following questions:

1. What are some specific lived experiences members of the team have had that have shaped them or had a significant impact on their world views?

2. What emotions came up for me during these months of self-assessment?

3. How have my personal experiences, beliefs, and personality shaped how I think about empathy?

4. How have my personal experiences, beliefs, and personality shaped how I think about power?

5. Based on my journaling exercises in the chapter about power and shadow power, what kinds of shadow powers am I (and my team) bringing to the table?

6. Where do I/my team believe I fall on the empathy and power continuum? (pg. 117)

7. Where do I/my team believe I/we fall on the empathy and power continuum as a team prior to starting this work vs. after doing the self-reflections and book exercises? Based on the team's conversation, identify three priority action steps you can take as a team to start to move the work forward.

8. Who will hold me/my team accountable as I/we move forward in the work of balancing empathy and power?

We can't work to correct imbalances in our teams or in others until we have first done the work in ourselves. As you complete this part of the journey, cultivate mindfulness to recognize internal resistance or defensiveness. If you find yourself (or your team) thinking things like, "But, I'm a nice and good person," or "Why would they say that about me?" or "Clearly, I'm not built for this based on this assessment," or any self-deprecating talk, interrupt it immediately. That language is defeatist and gives power away. We can't make excuses or walk away from our own work if we want to help correct it in our teams or in the greater community outside of us.

Summarizing Phase One: Begin Within

Goal: Examine your emotions, biases, and positionality before engaging with others.

+ Recognize your own perceptions and experiences by journaling
+ Participate in as many assessments as possible to gain a holistic understanding of oneself
+ Reflect on your lived experiences and assessment results
+ Identify where empathy and power dynamics intersect in your own life
+ Identify the priority action for yourself or your team to move forward

B.L.U.E. Phase Two: Learn & Locate
Time: 3-6 months, 2 Quarters

This second phase of the process is for investigating any imbalances in yourself, your team, and/or the group for whom you are seeking change. This step could take a decent chunk of time. I would consider at least one to two full business quarters (3-6 months) or more. Why would this take such a significant amount of time? It involves direct interviews with employees/ members, reporting data, and completing lengthy questions about the state of your environment. For an individual or small team (under 10 people), you can estimate on the smaller end of that time range, but for larger teams or for the investigation of groups outside of your team, it will take much longer to acquire information.

In this phase, you will use the information you gained in the first step about yourself and the introductory portion of sharing with a team, and move a step further into the investigation of others, systems, and processes in your environment. It is in this phase that you will deepen your understanding (learn) of where the imbalance occurs in others (locate). The reason this step takes a bit more time is that truths are uncovered, team contradictions may occur, and real vulnerabilities within the organization may be exposed. This step is not for the faint of heart. Your own levels of power and empathy will be challenged, and your own perceptions of yourself, the organization, systems, and processes may change—and change is hard. The purpose of this step is to change our behaviors and how we work, and lead others as well as ourselves. Your work environment, meaning the ways of working in your organization, will be assessed, evaluated, and changed. This will require reading through policies, human resources practices, procedures, handbooks, engagement surveys, and data insights from previous data collections about the organization. It could also mean reading reports and memos about organizational successes, having conversations with others, and more.

If you are completing this work with a team, some of the work involved in this step takes quite a bit of research, consolidation, and communication of the information in a way that everyone on the working team can digest and use to move forward. Some of the best ways to get some of this information are in confidential interviews. For some organizations that have built a culture of trust, it may be easier to acquire, but for others that have a damaged culture, expect resistance and fear. There are mechanisms that can help in acquiring information when people are afraid to be vulnerable or share their feedback. This is the stage where the following can be helpful:

+ Interviews, focus groups, or conversations across the organization, team, or community
+ Third-party survey tools for feedback (ensures confidentiality)

- ✦ Investigating the opposite point of view as if studying for a debate
- ✦ Tools for recording high volumes of information
- ✦ Utilize a secure AI platform to analyze notes or consolidate information. (Note: if you choose to do this, be careful about how you prompt the platform and what details are edited out that will not provide context and human voice to the feedback.)

It is important throughout this detailed step that you are in the role of investigation, not judgment. Judgment of others is indicative of a shadow power related to personal well-being and gets into the ego. If you collect information and judge others in the process, it will block your ability to gather accurate insights. Remember that everyone's experiences lead them to make specific decisions. In the words of Don Miguel Ruiz, "nothing others say or do is because of you," so try not to take anything personally and try very hard not to sit in judgment. The goal is not to scold someone for where they sit on the continuum, but to identify how to change behaviors so that you, the team, system, or organization as a whole can shift back into a balance.

If you are working with a team, it may be a good idea to set a working agreement around trusting others on your team to pay attention to what is said when information is being uncovered and to call out times when judgmental statements are made. These would be statements like, "What is wrong with these people? I can't believe this was happening and they did nothing?" or "Wow, no wonder no one listens to her, she's clueless" or "This is the dumbest policy I've ever seen in a work environment." While we all have real emotions, remember that a part of empathy is self-regulation.

If you are working alone, try to take notes or jot down when these thoughts creep into your mind or when you say them out loud. Write them down in a place you will see again to remind yourself to try not to do it as you continue working. Keep in mind how you are remaining in control of your own emotions and empathy throughout this step.

How you start this part of the process is dependent on the goal you are trying to accomplish, whether the goal is for yourself or others, to move levels of empathy or move levels of power.

Please note:

+ If you are doing this work for yourself, proceed with the steps below.
+ If you are doing this work with a small team, create a timeline for gathering information, sharing insights, and drafting conclusions.
+ If you are doing this work for a larger group or community, assign roles and responsibilities to teammates, as well as create a timeline for gathering information, sharing insights, and drafting conclusions.

Learn and Locate for Individuals

Below are investigative questions for individuals to help you learn and locate the imbalance of power and empathy in your life:

+ What didn't I know about myself that I discovered through the exercises in the book, and throughout the collection of data?
+ Have I included the perception and insight of others in my discovery of self?
+ How do the opinions and insights of others influence my own empathy and power?
+ What evidence is there of an imbalance between empathy and power in my life? What qualities or symptoms arise as a result of the imbalance?
+ Where do I think I fall on the power and empathy continuums? Do others think I fall in the same or different areas?
+ Are the imbalances different at work versus at home?
+ Are there rules or systems that I have set up for myself that perpetuate the imbalance?
+ Am I surrounding myself with others who push or pull the imbalance in one direction or another?
+ If I am leaning too heavily in one direction, what resources can I find to assist in supporting the work needed to balance?

Learn and Locate for Teams

For teams investigating their own imbalance, read through the expectations of the work and the suggested timeframe for this work, and create a timeline for when you want this work to be completed in each phase, like a project plan. The time is dependent on how your team works together. If you are a fast-working team, your timelines may be more aggressive, but if you want to create more time for processing and discussion, your timeline may be a little longer. Don't get too hung up on time more than accomplishing the goals of the work. After the timeline has been set by the team leader or chair, begin to make time to have discussions around the following questions, and make sure to record notes:

✦ Whose voices are missing from the team, and how can they be included?

✦ Have we conducted team listening sessions to determine if there is information about our team or organization that reveals potential blind spots?

✦ How do you know there is an imbalance of empathy and power on your team? What qualities or symptoms are arising as a result of the imbalance?

✦ How has everyone on the team defined the imbalance? Refer to the continuum and create alignment.

✦ Who is experiencing the imbalance? Is it a specific person on the team? Is it the team's view of the organization?

✦ Are there systems or processes set up in the team or in the organization that perpetuate the imbalance?

✦ Have we asked others outside of the team for their perception on the imbalance? If yes, what were the results of that investigation? If not, what can we do to acquire that information?

✦ Is the team surrounded by others that push or pull the imbalance in one direction or another?

✦ If the team is leaning too heavily in one direction, what additional resources can be found to assist in supporting the work needed to balance?

Learn and Locate for Larger Teams/Communities

Larger teams or communities present many more variables that need to be considered and accounted for in this process. It is important to have a working leadership team assigned to specific roles similar to what you may find on a formal board, like: recording secretary, corresponding secretary, communications chair, lead co-chairs, etc. The roles or titles can be unique to your organization or community and should make the most sense for your culture. This team should have no more than ten people. More than that causes the duplication of work tasks, could slow down the work, and compromises confidentiality when required. The most important part of working with larger groups is ensuring that the information gathered is recorded, analyzed, and shared with the larger group along the way. Communicating the why at critical points in the process may also be important to ensure you understand the process by members of the organization or community. Use the following questions to help guide the conversation and receive feedback.

+ Based on what you have learned in the assessments you've taken as a team and the deep dive in the data, what gaps were uncovered related to culture, power dynamics, engagement, employee sentiment, and more from the organization, team, or community you're in?

+ Whose voices may not be present on the team, how can they be included? What is the benefit of including those voices?

+ How do you know there is an imbalance of empathy and power? What qualities or symptoms are arising as a result of the imbalance?

+ How can we include others in defining the imbalance? (ex, does education need to happen on this topic?)

+ Who is experiencing the imbalance? Is it one specific person or a group?

+ Is the imbalance inside the organization or outside the

organization? If outside, where do you find reputable and reliable information about the group or person experiencing the imbalance?

+ Are there systems or processes set up inside or outside of the organization that perpetuate the imbalance?

+ Have we asked others outside of the organization or in the community for their perception on the imbalance? If yes, what were the results of that investigation? If not, what can we do to acquire that information?

+ Is the team or organization surrounded by others that push or pull the imbalance in one direction or another?

+ If the larger team or organization is leaning too heavily in one direction (either empathy or power), what additional resources can be found to assist in supporting the work needed to balance?

Third, gather the information and compile it into a usable document or report that can be shared among the working team for the next step in the process. This is different for every organization. For some, it could be a slide deck, for others, it could be tables, graphs, and images, and for others, it could be an organized multi-paged report. It is dependent on how people best receive, interpret, and use information in that setting.

Fourth, review the final draft. Go back through the information and ask a trusted advisor (this could be a supervisor, a senior leader, or a community leader) that is not on the team the following questions:

+ What is not in the report that should be to enhance understanding?

+ Is anyone's voice not accounted for in the report?

+ Is anything confusing or vague?

+ What would make the report better?

+ Is there any potential for bias in the report? Where?

+ Could the validity of the report be challenged, and why?

+ What may help senior leaders take action as a result of the findings?

These questions will help the team to deepen the legitimacy and validity of the information in the report prior to building a plan of action.

Summarizing Phase Two: Learn and Locate

Goal: Actively seek out diverse perspectives, challenge assumptions, and deepen understanding.

✦   Examine structural and systemic factors that influence the imbalance

✦   Engage in dialogue that centers the voices of those with different lived experiences.

✦   Investigate the imbalances, where it is located and in whom.

✦   Seek tools to enhance understanding.

✦   Consolidate information and validate the legitimacy of the information.

B.L.U.E. Phase Three: Unify and Build
Time: Varies (Minimum 6 months to 3 years depending on the extent of the imbalance)

The third phase of this process is important because it outlines *how* you will tackle the imbalance between empathy and power and begin to solve for it. Note that the first word in this phase is Unify. If the goal of this is not simply for self, and you are working on a team or for a larger community, the team must be unified in its mission, goals, and information up to this point. There is no possible way any plan that is created will be successful if every single person is not unified in its overall purpose. This does not mean that every person on the team will support every outcome or decision for how this will get done, but they must live with it (recall from the home group/task group story). There must be a level of agreement and unity.

If the process is carried out with a balance of empathy and power for all involved, this shouldn't be an issue. Whenever I lead a presentation or project, I never do anything that I wouldn't also expect of my team or others. Lead by modeling and by example for the outcome of the project. It would be a less-than-satisfactory outcome if, after completing the plan and doing all of this work, someone identifies an imbalance between empathy and power in the working team or its team leader. Yikes! #fail #backtothedrawingboard

This phase of the process is also where creativity, branding, and outcomes are specific to your team, organization and community, if working within one. Yet, another reason I would not put a specific solution in this book is because I have zero knowledge of the brand, language, and impact needed to draft a solution for every individual, group, team, organization, and community. This is another reason why one size fits all does not work.

Rather than a step-by-step process in this phase, I will outline what the to-dos are for your team. Think of this as a checklist. Do not forget to refer to the elements of the blueprint in the next chapter for this step, which illustrate what needs to happen while drafting and creating the plan. The outcome of this phase is to build a unified strategy and plan that will solve the imbalance. You want a plan that will:

☐   Align with both/and thinking. You may want to use the book, *Navigating Polarities*, as your template for decision making. This should not be the solution you use to identify imbalances and solve for others, yet it is a way for you to work through the issues or contradictory ideas and approaches inside the working team.

☐   Address the root cause of the imbalance. If symptoms exist, are there any that need immediate attention? Look back at the previous chapters at what can result from imbalances between empathy and power. Serious symptoms may be behavior that is causing harm to individuals or teams, or leading to poor decision-making that affects the overall health of the organization.

☐   Ensure that actions address both personal growth and systemic change for all involved.

☐ Include education of others, which is where the interviews and other actions named above in the investigation phase come in.

☐ Detail sustainable, measurable outcomes. Use the SMART rule when outlining outcomes: Specific, Measurable, Attainable, Relevant and Timely. For example, we will interview 10% of the employee population to identify gaps in empathy and power dynamics by April 15.

☐ Remove or call attention to the team's own bias as much as possible by doing as much work up front to identify some of those biases with the assessments listed.

☐ Allow for change and adaptability (for example, how will you modify or shift to plan B if needed?)

☐ Be simple to understand, especially if for a community or a leader. If the plan or actionable steps aren't clear or are too difficult to execute, it will be rejected.

☐ Address whether money or cost is involved. If so, where will that money come from? What will it go towards? Why is that necessary (or not)?

☐ Identify resources needed to shift the outcome from intent to active impact.

☐ Identify who needs to be involved in executing the actions and who (externally) will remain involved for accountability.

☐ Anticipate communication that is needed, in what formats, and to whom it needs to be communicated.

☐ List the long-term positive effects of the work on the organization, team, or community.

When you draft an action plan, you want that plan to resonate with those who are engaging with it and those who are receiving it for the first time. One of the ways that I have found best to think about this is using a research-based approach for whole brain thinking. The research on whole-brain thinking was developed by William Hermann.[41] If you chose to take the HBDI Assessment for whole brain thinking, then you have already seen an example of his work in action for yourself and your working team. His approach addressed solutions, not just with the parts of our brain that we use most often, the parts that we prefer, or the parts that we have strengths in, but to stretch ourselves to use the other parts of the brain as well. I have used this in my work as a leader to help create better or more inclusive meetings, improve meeting efficiencies, and create better working environments. Simply identifying how people think helps to create better working relationships. If you approach the draft of the plan and communication for your plan with the following framework, it will help develop a more well-rounded approach that is capable of more to understand:

+ What? What results are we trying to achieve? (Data)
+ Why? Why is this solution needed or important to accomplish? (Vision)
+ How? How are we going to accomplish the goals? (Plans)
+ Who? Who will be involved, and who will be impacted by the outcome? (Feeling)

The rest of the process is dependent on great project management skills, relationship-building, trust, and all of the other aspects that are independent of a solution for this specifically and more related to great organizational development. Do not forget to adjust for equitable practices, inclusive processes, and decisions that are both ethical and effective (both/and thinking). Once you have completed this phase, do the same thing that you did in the previous phase and rely on trusted advisors outside of the team to be your checks and balances for the following questions:

+ What is not in the plan that should be to enhance understanding?
+ Is anyone's voice not accounted for in the plan?
+ Is anything confusing or vague?
+ What would make the plan better?
+ Is there any potential for bias in the plan? Where?
+ Could the validity of the plan be challenged, and why?

If you are looking for a more practical application of what this could look like, I will share how I went about creating a successful mentoring and sponsorship program. While I will not reveal all of the details of the program because they are owned by that business, I will share the steps I used and why it was successful. You will find that at the end of Chapter 11.

Summarizing Phase Three: Unify and Build

Goal: Create a plan that is unified, equitable and exhibits the unique creativity and branding specific to you (or your team / organization / community):

+ Develop action plans that incorporate what you have learned
+ Commit to making decisions that use both / and thinking
+ Navigate polarities in thought and opinion
+ Use whole-brain thinking to address action steps
+ Check your own imbalances through the process
+ Ensure actions address both individual and systemic needs

E – Enact and Nurture (Sustained Growth & Adaptation)
Time: Ongoing

This fourth and final phase of the process is all about enacting what you have planned, assessing its impact and then nurturing the sustainability of the work.

There isn't too much to say about putting your plan into action because it is your plan. You built it, now get it done.

What I can also do is motivate you with one of my dad's favorite quotes:

"If a task is once begun, never leave it 'til it's done.
Be the task great or small, do it well or not at all."
~Author Unknown

While the original author is unknown, the legendary musician, producer, director and composer, Quincy Jones, Jr., is most credited with saying it because his father said it to him. I am almost certain this is where my father heard it as well, because he loved Quincy Jones.

No matter what the plan is, if you build it using what you have learned throughout the book while listening to the voices of others and balancing them with your own power, it will be successful. You must have supreme leadership skills if you are enacting this plan for others. You also must have an accountability circle that will keep you grounded (and the team, if not for yourself only).

After you have implemented the plan, nurturing the plan is essential. When the plan is a success, you should take time to acknowledge that and celebrate it! It is hard work to make these kinds of changes, whether in yourself or for a whole team or company. When that celebration ends, the long-term work begins. This journey is a marathon, not a sprint. It is life-long. As we have seen so often, people start with the best intentions and they act on them accordingly, and all it takes is one slip, one trauma, one unexpected turn, and the entire blueprint can come tumbling down.

Nurturing the plan means constantly reflecting on the outcomes of your actions, relentlessly focused on remaining as balanced as you can for yourself and for your team in any given moment, remaining open to feedback and growth, and maintaining an environment that fosters vulnerability and accountability. A lasting change will not last without adjusting and adapting over time. You see, we are dealing with human products that all have minds of their own and free will. We are not dealing with an inanimate object or a non-feeling, non-thinking being. Humans can shift on a dime sometimes with no warning because of their own life experiences and this includes you! That is why having a system in place for checks and balances and accountability are so important in this work.

What does nurturing mean? Bring back those assessments you started with and do them again annually or bi-annually! Start a new journal and go back through the self-evaluation after a major life event, whether it was perceived as a negative or positive one. Regardless of if the life experience is life-changing or minimal, it could have a tremendous impact on your viewpoint, or your teams. Keep in check with your team members, employees, or other involved parties to see if what was planned was working.

Here are some good self-check questions to incorporate if you haven't thought of them already in your plan for sustainability:

✦ If you get new team members or new community members, how will you get them up to speed?

✦ What is working and what isn't when it comes to balancing the level of empathy and power?

✦ How will you collect regular feedback from those involved in the change and those impacted by the change?

✦ How can you ensure feedback is considered, valued and used to make adjustments?

✦ Who is going to hold you accountable as an individual? Who will hold the team accountable?

✦ How will you get support when needed? How will the team support one another through any potential changes?

✦ How do you maintain momentum and morale when it gets difficult, or the team is overwhelmed with other tasks?

✦ When is it time to seek help from outside of myself, the team, or the organization?

✦ What happens if there is a shift in the senior positions of leadership?

✦ What is the evidence that there's a balance of empathy and power? What is the evidence that there isn't?

These are all questions that can lead you down a path of accountability, nurturing and sustainability of your action plan. As you move forward, feel confident that you have checked every box, and examined it from every angle. Congratulations!

Summarizing Phase Four: Enact and Nurture

Goal: Continuously assess, refine, and nurture your actions and strategies with accountability and attainable measures.

✦ Reflect on the outcomes of your actions and adjust as needed.
✦ Stay open to growth, knowing this is an evolving process.
✦ Foster a culture of accountability and long-term change.
✦ Regularly evaluate how your choices influence others.
✦ Stay open to feedback and potential change.
✦ Nurture long-term sustainability of team or relationships with self.

As you begin each phase, the following chapters will help you with the approach and the conceptual understanding of the blueprint. Afterwards, there is further discussion about potential limitations depending on your sector, particularly if you are completing these activities with a team. The final chapters will be dependent on information most relevant to the year of publication (2025), and this should be kept in mind as policies and laws change with a new presidential cabinet as well as social and community issues that are ever evolving. Just as these factors are ever-changing, so will your plan need to adapt and change or even be ready to anticipate future twists and turns that affect us all personally and professionally. This chapter has tackled the question: what do I do to fix this? The next chapter will answer the question: how do I think about this to lead the work?

CHAPTER 9

From Framework to Mindset

Now that you have an understanding of the work that needs to be done and the elements of the B.L.U.E.Print © steps that will help you outline the work, it's time to visualize and conceptualize how to remember and think about each of the steps in the process.

Creating the Blueprint Mindset

You have probably seen a blueprint or two in your life in various forms. A blueprint is like a floor plan of a house, building, or structure. When an architect draws up a design of a building or structure, they create a very detailed drawing of the rooms, the stairs, the windows, the walls, literally everything that is included in the building. If you have ever built a home or moved into an apartment, you may have seen the basic floor plans that are drawn. More basic versions of these floor plans are often posted to apartment websites or home realty sites so that a potential renter or buyer can get an idea of the design.

It is called a blueprint because the actual final drawing and design is printed on a special, sturdy paper called vellum. This type of paper is made from a historical process, and it leaves the paper blue with white lines. Those white lines are the design lines. I use this blueprint analogy to prepare you for how you think about your plan design—but these plans are to fix the imbalance of empathy and power.

And finally, I wanted to provide context for the approach that was comprehensive, like how a blueprint is comprehensive and a layout of the whole building being built. Getting to the root cause of an imbalance between empathy and power must be addressed from every angle. Just as you read about all of the intricacies of empathy and power in the previous chapters, you completed the work individually and/or with a team, and learned how someone can get out of balance with either empathy or power. You tackled this work comprehensively. In order to know how to approach it from every angle, it helps to have a visual to shape your approach and thinking, as well as how to lead yourself (and your team) through the work. It also helps to have mechanisms for remembering your design approach, which is what you will receive in this chapter. This is not the solution, yet this is a way to help guide you through the journey of balancing empathy and power.

The Memory Palace

Many people have utilized or heard of various memorization techniques or ways to commit things to memory. The most common method used by educators and students, even in my own experience as an educator for 17 years, is the mnemonic device, where you take a series of letters from what you need to remember and create a saying, sentence, or memorable phrase. I remember when I was learning to play the piano and learning the note letters of the treble clef lines: EGBDF - Every Good Boy Does Fine. Mnemonic devices obviously work for me because I have remembered that for decades. You can also refer to the use of the mnemonic device in the word B.L.U.E. as the steps of the actionable work that needs to be done, as you saw in the previous chapter. Similarly, the memory palace technique will help you remember what needs to happen as you are using the Balance B.L.U.E.Print © framework front and center in your mind.

The memory palace is credited to an ancient Greek poet, Simonides of Ceos, who lived during 556 BC.[42] The short version of the story is that Simonides was at a banquet hall reciting a poem, but left the banquet hall for a short time. While he was gone, the roof fell in, tragically killing everyone inside. When he returned, he was able to identify all of the victims because he had remembered them based on where they were sitting—or their loci (location). The other name for the memory palace is "method of loci." The science behind this method is that by associating a new or unfamiliar idea with a familiar location or place, it is easier to understand and commit the idea to memory. Many of us choose the same grocery store to shop in for this reason -- because we remember the location of the items we need. You may hear this spoken of loosely as having a photographic memory. Just think about a time when your favorite grocery store or place to shop reorganized all of the product aisles and shelves and you can no longer quickly locate things when you shop!

A way to practically use this method, perhaps one more applicable, is to assign items in your house to ideas, concepts, or items you need to remember. For example, if I were a medical student studying the pathway of blood through the heart as it enters and exits the lungs, I would think of a room in my house to represent various parts of the process and help me remember the blood's pathway. Here's how that would look:

✦ My front door is the Vena Cava: De-oxygenated blood enters the heart through the Vena Cava.

✦ I walk from the kitchen (right atrium) into the dining room (right ventricle): Blood enters the right atrium, then through a valve goes into the right ventricle.

✦ I walk from the dining room (right ventricle) out the patio doors (pulmonary artery) to the deck for fresh air (lungs): The blood exits the heart to the lungs via the pulmonary artery.

✦ I walk back into the house to the living room patio entrance (left atrium) and into the garage (left ventricle) to load boxes into my car. Oxygenated blood then enters the left atrium then through a valve to the left ventricle.

✦ I get into my car (Aorta) and pull out of the garage to deliver the boxes: The oxygenated blood leaves via the aorta, which carries the oxygen to the rest of the body.

While this example seems involved, the next time I need to recall the flow of blood or the names of the parts of the body involved, I can now just think about my own house. If I think of the front door, I immediately know that's the Vena Cava. If I think of the patio, I know I'm getting air in the lungs. The memory palace is the process of assigning a concept to something familiar, helping it remain transfixed in our memory just as our home is.

The visual concept is organized so the steps in the process can be remembered—the more you are able to recall and understand the steps, the more likely it will be for you to uphold them as well as pass them on to the people who need to hear and understand them.

Mindset Elements

In a blueprint for a home, you find structural dimensions like the walls, windows, support structures, stairs and foundation, the details for the measurements for the rooms of the house, additional levels like a second floor loft or landing overlook, and the external appearance of the home, like the front door, a patio, and even the walkway leading up to the house (if it is asked for in the design). I will use each of the features of a house to help you remember how to approach the steps in the B.L.U.E.Print©. In the following sub-sections, you will notice an initial and words in parentheses following each subtitle. These align the action steps to the blueprint, which I described in Chapter 8.

You may find it helpful to refer to the diagram of the blueprint while following along in the explanation of each element. I am a visual learner, so I fully understand the need for a picture or visual to assist.

KEY:

① The Foundation
② Walkway
③ Front Door
④ Entry
⑤ Great Room with a half wall
⑥ Windows
⑦ Stairs
⑧ Balcony/Loft
⑨ Dimensions

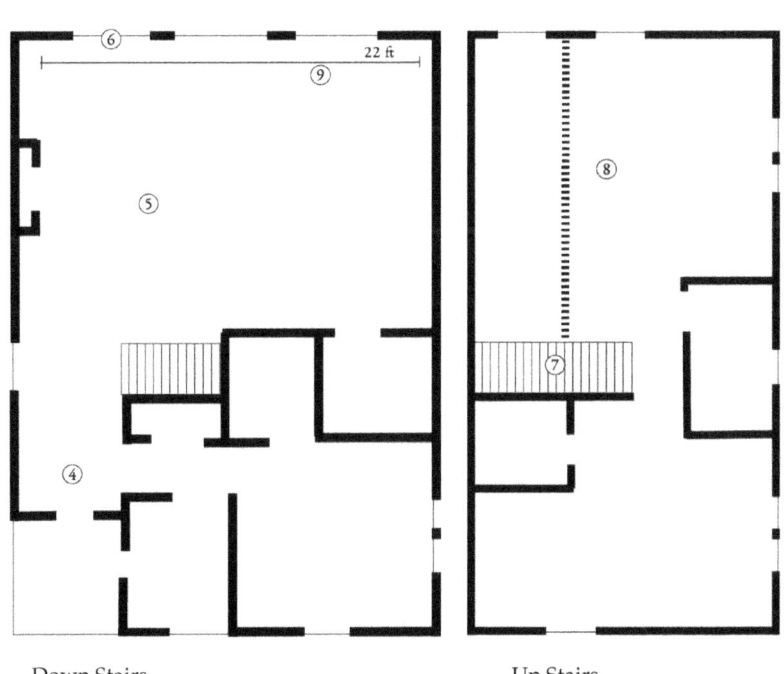

Down Stairs   Up Stairs

① The Foundation - Ensuring your foundational knowledge is sound and intact

② Walkway - Observing the issue from the outside

③ Front Door - Identifying the approach and who is on the journey with you

④ Entry - Standing in the problem and identifying which way to go

⑤ Great Room with a half wall - Working on Empathy or Power (or both)

⑥ Windows - Remember to pay attention to what is happening outside

⑦ Stairs - Climbing up to a higher level of understanding

⑧ Balcony/Loft - Observing from the top down to see all sides of the issues

⑨ Dimensions - Measuring success and balance

The Foundation (B - Begin Within)

Before a house is built, you must know what it's going to be built on to ensure the house will stand. Similarly, before you approach the imbalance of power and empathy, you need to be sure that your own foundational knowledge of self and others has been completed, which means reading the chapters about empathy and power, doing the exercises, investigating your own areas of improvement, and analyzing your team, your organization, and business. You finish this by practicing self-awareness and accountability. If you skip this part of the process, the rest of your journey will be exceedingly difficult and more likely to fail, much like one crack in the foundation can mean impending danger to the stability of the rest of the house.

You must hold yourself accountable to learning as much as possible about empathy and power for yourself and your team members (if applicable) first.

The previous chapters have led you through the activities needed to start this work, but if you skipped over anything, need a refresh, or thought some activities weren't necessary, go back before continuing forward.

Walkway (L - Learn & Locate)

Whenever I walk up to a new home, I usually look around at the surroundings, the landscape, and the outside of the house to take it all in. I make some decisions on how I approach the front door based on what I observe. If I see an unkempt lawn, cracked paint, broken windows, and dead flowers, I might decide the house is spooky and I approach with caution. If I see a fresh garden, a well-landscaped lawn, friendly decorations at the door, and signs of kindness, I may approach with excitement. We can make quick judgments about people, just like we do when we pull up in front of a house that we are cautious of, and those judgments may not be accurate to your interpretations, but they do dictate how people move forward.

The walkway symbolizes what you initially observe about the self, a person, a group, a team, or a community in which the imbalance exists, so that you know how to best approach them when you are ready to solve the imbalance. Remember that as you approach, you may be entering a conversation or observation with your own preconceived notions. Keep your mind open and be willing to be wrong about any pre-judgments you may have made. Making that effort will go a long way to reducing any bias you are bringing to the next steps.

Front Door (L - Learn & Locate)

This is one of the most important parts of the framework. You must walk right into the front door, or the location of the imbalance, and do so with confidence, or perhaps caution, depending on your walkway experience. Remember that if you want to ensure a change in correcting the imbalance of empathy and power, the door must be opened for you. The door in this circumstance is the invitation or acceptance of another person or group of people to allow the work to happen.

There might be someone waiting at the door to open it for you. Maybe it's someone asking you to join them on this journey of healing division through balancing power and empathy. Or maybe you are opening the door for yourself, brave but alone. Maybe you have walked up to the door with someone else—a manager, a coworker, a friend, or maybe you are approaching the door and the person on the other side is resistant to letting you in. Either way, you must boldly walk through this front door, and in some circumstances, have patience to wait for the door to open, ready to locate and reconcile the imbalance.

Think of a person, or a group of people, in your life, team, or organization who is likely to open the door for you. They may open the door for the discussion, or you may have to push the door open wider to walk in yourself. For example, if you are a leader, you may have a direct report that requires some coaching. You know from experience that initially they may be quiet or seem resistant, but as you talk and continue to explain and open the door a little wider, their mood softens, and it doesn't take long for them to receive your feedback. They open the door. If you are an employee giving feedback to your manager, it may take more risk in certain organizational structures, but if trust and safety are built into the relationship, you may just have to say what needs to be said. You push just a little, and the door opens. Sometimes you have to ask to come in, and sometimes the door will fly open, and someone will stand with open arms and excitement to let you in. You must be prepared for any of those scenarios to occur. If you force your way into any type of behavior change in another person, group, team, or community, be prepared to be met with resistance or equal force. Humor me here and let me drive this point home a little bit more because this step is crucial for success.

When I was a kid, I loved watching a popular family sitcom on Thursday evenings with my parents. In one episode, one of the daughters brought home a new boyfriend who turned out to be a much older fiancée and who worked at her college, and all of this information was a surprise to her parents. Her parents, while as polite as possible, were very upset with their daughter, and eventually, at the dinner table, the daughter expressed her frustration about how they were being treated. The father interrupted her and, in so many words, said, "If you prepare an expensive five-star meal and then serve it on a used garbage can lid, no one will eat it."

If you offer someone their favorite dessert and then smash it in their face, or try to force them to eat it, they will spit it back out at you. It does not matter how enticing your reason, research, or purpose is; if the person is not ready for it, the door will remain shut, and you will have a difficult time making progress. This step is important because you may have to visit several times before someone opens the door. At this step, you are working on how to prepare for that if the person or people you need to address are not ready to let you in.

Entry (L - Learn and Locate)

Once inside a house for the first time, I always stop in the entry and look around and take in all of the sights, sounds, and smells. I look around at the layout of the house and peek inside the rooms if I'm able to do so politely. The entry is your opportunity to observe the imbalance from inside of yourself, the team, or the community. In this step, you will gather more evidence about whether the imbalance is tipping towards too much empathy or too much power. This step is investigative, and there should be many questions involved in determining which "room" you will start in first. It will also be crucial to set the tone for your own role in moving forward. Think of a person who comes to your house with a gift and is extremely friendly, versus someone who comes to your house and is immediately accusatory, critical, or negative. You'd like to tell that person to leave. You do not want to be that person in this scenario. As you enter the home and look around, consider how you're entering.

The Great Room (U - Unify and Build)

Many of the modern-day homes have scrapped the old floor plans where every room was separate and had a doorway to walk through to get to that room. Gone is the old notion of hiding in the kitchen so as not to expose disorder or preparation. The concept of the Great Room allows everyone to stay together while providing different functionalities. A great room is a huge open space, but typically separated into a living room or dining area and the kitchen. The great room is also typically where everyone gathers to socialize, eat, relax, and do a multitude of activities. The open space allows for two or more functional opportunities at the same time. Gasp! Did I just allude that two things can be true in one open space?! Empathy and Power are the Great Room. These two concepts, while separate, must coexist and work together in an open space at the same time, just like a great room. If you need to visualize this, you can assign either empathy or power to the kitchen side versus the living room side.

Once you have investigated whether you need to concentrate your work on empathy or power first (the kitchen or the living room inside of the great room), it doesn't mean that you can take your eyes and concentration off of the other completely. For example, maybe your team is exceedingly more empathetic, and the work you concentrate on first with them is to realize the team's power. However, this does not mean you stop being empathetic altogether. You must also think about your levels of empathy at the same time. It is just like a great room, when you enter the kitchen, while keeping your eyes on the other side of the room, where the family is hanging out in the living room. It is very important for you to stay vigilant, just as a hostess would if she were in the kitchen prepping an appetizer and ensuring her children were behaving themselves. This step is where the majority of the work is done.

Windows (E - Enact and Nurture)

Is it getting a little stuffy in that great room? Feeling a little boxed in? Well, open a window! Just like when we are inside our own houses, it can get a little stuffy, you might hear some concerning noises outside, or you just need some fresh air. When you are working hard on correcting this imbalance, it may take more time than you think, and there may be times when you have to come up for air and take a break. The window could symbolize this for you. You may be hard at work, and someone from outside the team or an external force could distract the work. You may have to pause the work to observe the distraction and determine if it is something that affects you directly or if it is an actual sign of danger. The window could symbolize this for you. Think of the window as your way to observe the outside or to take a pause and recharge. You might reach out to an "outside" source for advice or insight. This step is important for self-care and to protect the integrity of the work you are doing to correct the imbalance between empathy and power.

Dimensions (E - Enact and Nurture)

Every aspect of a blueprint has dimensions, or the measurements needed to build a safe and secure structure. For the sake of our analogy and memory palace, we will loosely interpret the symbolism of dimensions because, in a real blueprint, the dimensions are set before the house is built. However, the dimensions are also added to the design as they are being created and refined, and that is how we are going to think of it for the Balance B.L.U.E.Print ©. After you have identified what needs to be corrected and have developed a plan to do so, you must determine what measures indicate a safe, secure, and successful balance. Remember that the overall goal of this work is to restore unity and balance between empathy and power, so the measures you use to determine that the balance is reached are key. It should be noted that these dimensions may change, as opposed to the dimensions of a real blueprint, because you are attempting to correct imbalances in human behavior, which are not static like a building structure. It is ever-changing. Be ready to shift if needed on this very important goal-setting part of the blueprint.

Stairs (U - Unify and Build)

There aren't always stairs in every house, but stairs exist in the Balance B.L.U.E.Print © house. There is always a second level in our house because you must be able to go up to look down. Stairs symbolize the ability to take you up to higher ground or back down to the ground level. This is the point at which you have to step away from being a part of the work and observe how the team is working. It means investigating whether or not something is missing or if the work is heading in the right or wrong direction, similar to being at a real party and knowing you need to head upstairs to the balcony to see the entire party all at once.

While working on your plan, you may have to look at the problem from various angles, and if you are on the ground level doing the work, it may be difficult to see everything that is happening. If you, your team, or others doing the work with you are experiencing frustration and you have already used the window, it may be time for you to step away and look at the work from a visionary perspective. To do that, you have to exit the ground level, which can be difficult because it may mean not doing the work *with* your team for a short time as you step out to observe the team. This can make you (and your team) nervous, or it could be just what you (and your team) need to do. If you have built trust and solid relationships with your team, you should be able to work through this without any trouble. This step represents the pathway and the journey of climbing to another level of understanding. Sometimes it is really difficult to take the stairs because you don't want to leave your team or make them feel like you have abandoned their work, but on your way up, you think and continue to move. Climbing the stairs in this case means getting quiet and realizing that as a leader, you may not be able to be "on the ground" with the employees or team as the work is getting done. You have to climb up to a balcony level to see how to help.

Balcony/Loft (E - Enact and Nurture)

I do not have a loft in my house, but I do have a balcony. I have been in a house with a loft before, and it's always so fun to climb the stairs to stand up there. If a friend is hosting a party and I venture to the loft overlooking the living room area, I can see everything that is happening. Every time I have had the opportunity to do this, I always look first at the people I was just speaking with and then at those that were around me, and usually I learn something I would never have seen if I had stayed down on ground level. In one of my building assignments as an assistant principal, we would work bus duty and dismissal after school. One day, I was using my walkie-talkie to identify where the principal was because he was not visible at the bus line just outside of the school's front door. After I called for him on the walkie, he responded, "Look up." And there he was, on the roof of the one-story building, looking down on dismissal. My initial reaction was laughter, and he smiled too, but I remember asking him afterwards why he was up on the roof that day. He said that he was getting a new perspective, as it was difficult when on the ground to see where students collect or how they move after students were let out for dismissal.

160

The Balcony/Loft area of the Balance B.L.U.E.Print © house allows for leaders and independent thinkers to set a vision, anticipate future roadblocks, fix behaviors that are distracting from the work, and decide if it is time to concentrate on the other side of the great room. If, for example, you start correcting an empathy imbalance and notice the team has shifted to power struggles, this is how you step up to identify that shift. It is hard to notice if you, too, are on ground level with them. If you are doing this work individually, this is the point at which you identify and lean into an accountability partner to check your perspectives and direction.

Whenever you are stuck with how to think about the work, this layout will help to clear that up. You can visualize the house and think, "Where are we in the house right now?"

CHAPTER 10:

Potential Obstacles and Limitations

As we navigate balancing empathy and power and working to be a part of healing the division we see in America and in the world, we must realize that nothing is the same in every environment. I am not a politician, and this book is nonpartisan. I am not a lawyer, a governmental, financial, or economic expert, or someone who would purport to know all there is to know about every nuance in every field or industry. I will leave that up to experts in each field. However, I am someone with life experiences in several different industries and sectors, and the designer of the Balance B.L.U.E.Print ©. I believe, when used correctly, it works regardless of the field in which you work. An important life lesson from my parents was "Never stop learning." I encourage you to use this book as your personal way to apply that lesson and to never stop learning about yourself and others. It is the only pathway to balancing empathy and power effectively.

Any time you engage in work that is human-centered, there will be different limitations, obstacles, and challenges no matter what work you are attempting to do. The limitations are unpredictable, yet we must try to do the best we can to anticipate them.

Whenever I have put together a project plan or designed something to put into place at work, the senior leaders always expected me to address this question (in addition to many others): What issues or complications may derail the project or hinder the goal?

The point of this question was not to predict failure before the project started; it was to anticipate what could come up so that there were ways to solve those issues before or when they did. No one can anticipate or predict everything, but trying to think ahead will save time and improve outcomes. This is where both/and thinking and doing the assessments really help in the process. This is also how working to foresee obstacles might save you some headache.

Let's examine some of the obstacles and how they differ from sector to sector. I'd like to reiterate that these obstacles are dependent on where we are right now in the year 2025 in America. There are various obstacles all over the world. Some of them will be similar, and some of them will be vastly different. For the sake of this book, we are focusing on America in the year 2025.

Obstacles Within For-Profit Private Business

Some may consider this sector to be the least limited because there are a lot more freedoms that exist in project creation and implementation in this sector, versus other sectors. For-profit private businesses are independent businesses that generate revenue but do not publicly trade stock. For example, the LEGO company, Kohler, the local kitchen and bathroom appliance manufacturer, and more. I have worked in the private for-profit sector for about five years. However, when it comes to company culture, engagement, employee experience, human resources, diversity, equity, inclusion, and belonging, there are some increased limitations on what can be said or done at various times in the fiscal year. This could be related to what happens outside of the business (political decisions, social issues, global economy, etc.) or what happens in the scope of the business plans and strategy (i.e. how senior leaders are aware of a financial deficit and cut budget to fund the work).

While there are some laws and regulations that apply differently in this sector and may not be applicable or as strict, they certainly still affect what happens strategically or can increase risk. Risk is determined by specific departments in the business, which could be legal, finance, or HR. Usually, risk increases if the business is publicly traded, and stockholders and investors are involved (i.e., public companies). This is because the public has a share in the business, and what they desire can have positive or negative effects on the financial bottom line of the business. For those businesses and organizations that are for-profit, but not publicly traded, the freedoms do not include investors (private).

Sometimes, being a private business is a double-edged sword. The business can't run if it doesn't make financial sense to grow and employ more people, but the people are also who and what can improve business success. Additionally, the business won't run successfully if the people inside the business are running the business poorly. Financial success, in the for-profit world, is what drives strategy and ultimately prioritizes different kinds of work at any given time. So, if financial success is down, decisions to shift priorities and business goals around are commonplace. This is also dependent on senior leadership and the board of directors, which also applies to other sectors. The lack of financial success could become a limitation for project teams that have noticed issues in the balance of empathy and power in their teams or organizations, because it could limit the budget that is directed towards these projects and work, especially if senior leaders do not feel this work should be prioritized.

If the founding leader does not see a balance between empathy and power as important to pursue in their leadership style, this will most likely perpetuate the inequality within the company, and potentially create a culture of division further down the business timeline. Ironically, according to a 2023 article by Gallup, company profits increased by 85% in businesses with a strong, positive company culture.[43]

A final limitation that I have witnessed, but not encountered personally within the private, for-profit sector, is organizational structure. This may be independent of the influence of senior leadership. If a business does not have a central team that is strictly focused on maintaining and improving the employee experience, culture, or perhaps the creation of employee or business resource groups, then that could mean culture building is up to each individual team, or even sole individuals. This may mean that one or two people on each team are solely responsible for a heavy task, which on top of other duties and responsibilities becomes quite overwhelming and could prevent the completion of empathy versus power work or prevent this work from even starting at all.

Summary of For-profit Private Business Limitations:

✦ Financial success or loss can be a benefit to advocate for programs or initiatives, but can also be a limitation if priorities are shifted when profit is down.

✦ Leadership strategy and direction

✦ Misguided or disjointed organizational structures

Obstacles within Nonprofit Businesses

Private Sector

Some may be surprised to learn that not all nonprofit businesses are based on charitable giving from individuals or groups of people. Private nonprofit organizations are those that could be a foundation or funded by a single individual, family, or corporation. They can make grants to other organizations. An example of this would be the Bill and Melinda Gates Foundation, fraternities and sororities, alumni associations, and more. Because these are isolated to typically one person deciding where and how financial grants are given and to whom, one clear limitation is that if the person making the decisions has an empathy vs power imbalance, then the monies may not be used for repairing something that person is not interested in fixing. Recall the Power Tyrant. The financial donations may be made to people or organizations that perpetuate that divide.

Public Sector

Many of the same limitations above can exist in nonprofit businesses and organizations, like financial success or lack thereof, and organizational structure. However, in today's times, laws, regulations, and the overall mission of the nonprofit are the largest limiting factors. Currently, many nonprofits have lost federal grants and funding based on various presidential executive orders and state and local bills that have been passed in the legislature. In some cases, the limitations are related specifically to whom they serve, and in other cases, it may simply be because of their location in the country.

Unfortunately, the political nature of these decisions is causing financial difficulties for nonprofits as well because some people or for-profit businesses (who would have previously donated or sponsored nonprofit organizations) feel they are choosing between their belief systems, or their own financial worries and economic concerns. They may not understand the concept that two things can be true. For example, the current sitting president issued an executive order that prevents nonprofits that receive federal funding from receiving grants and contracts if they align with any efforts that relate to diversity, equity, inclusion, or accessibility, or have missions aligned with that work. This includes agencies like the YWCA, which has the mission to end racism, the National Public Radio, the Human Rights Campaign, and even Sesame Street. As a part of their annual giving campaigns, some major corporations may decide to withdraw their funding if they also receive government contracts or funding for fear of being targeted if they support the nonprofit. It is a ripple effect.

A statement from the National Council of Nonprofits (2025) read, "The work of charitable nonprofits covers a wide range of causes and efforts, and executive orders have the potential to impact funding, staffing, and general operations of critical community services…Staying abreast of the executive orders and their related actions is crucial for ensuring nonprofits are aware of upcoming hurdles to their work."

The work referred to here is mostly related to those whom they help or serve, but also relates to the staff who are employed to do the work as well. That could very well be you, and if that is the case, the imbalance may not lie *in* the organization, but lie *above* the organization itself, and that is a barrier that may be out of your span of control. It might be close to impossible to hold leaders above your own span of influence to a standard developed outside of your company.

Summary of Nonprofit Limitations:

✦ Legislation that inhibits funding to do the work of correcting imbalances

✦ Political ideologies and strategies to target those working to correct inequities

✦ Financial funding difficulties

✦ Leader beliefs and decisions

Education - Public Sector

The limitations of doing this work in the educational sector are very similar to those placed on nonprofits at this time in our political landscape, and in most cases are directly related to federal and state laws, regulations, and executive orders from the current presidential administration. Having said that, however, there are additional limitations in the public education sector that involve school district bureaucracies and district voters. This is not limited to schools that serve students ages three through eighteen, but also public colleges and universities.

Decisions that may prohibit the work of correcting an imbalance in empathy and power may occur regardless of the federal landscape and include how schools are funded by the states, as well as how well they are managed by state and local school boards across America. Some school funding formulas are based on property taxes, sales tax, state lottery systems, or toll fees. There are a variety of ways that school districts in America are funded.

There are also a variety of ways that schools are governed. In New York City public schools,[44] for example, there is a Chancellor who reports directly to the mayor. The Chancellor is the highest-ranking educational official in the NYC public schools, and that person manages the superintendents of each system of schools across the city. As of 2025, there are 45 superintendents of schools across the city that govern millions of students and hundreds of thousands of teachers. It is an enormous system of schools. In contrast, there is a small local school district in Dayton, Ohio, and the principals in the district all report to one superintendent who reports to the local school board.

What is consistent across all of these systems is that the positions of leadership, such as the school board, are elected by the people who live there.

While education is meant to be nonpartisan, you can imagine how the line is blurred when beliefs fuel decision-making and public beliefs affect who is voted into elected leadership positions at the top of the organizational chart.

Once again, the limitation of creating a formal plan to balance empathy and power in a school system may be related to actual legislation preventing that from happening, in which case it could be out of your control. However, it could be the system that you are attempting to overhaul if the policies, procedures, and ways of work are organized to perpetuate a divide or hierarchy that sustains an imbalance of empathy and power. In this case, the imbalance is so deeply embedded into the way the organization functions that it could mean a complete overhaul of how people work. Correcting an imbalance in a long-standing system will take a concerted effort and a very organized, methodical group of people over a longer period of time to see it through. It may be a long road, but it can be done!

Summary of Education Limitations:

+ Legislation that prohibits actions by employees of the school system
+ Those elected to leadership positions may be influenced by voters
+ Long-standing systematic policies and procedures that maintain a divide

Government/Military - Public Sector

I think it goes without saying that this may be the sector with the most limitations. This is most often because whatever is happening inside government systems directly rolls down into government teams, and the military is included in that. The military and some government teams and offices are also run on the status of power and rank where creativity, introduction of new ways of doing things, and new solutions are only allowable if a superior "allows" it. I have coached a coworker who entered the corporate environment after leaving the military from active duty. Let's call this person Harper. It took coaching and guidance, and perhaps a little bit of extra onboarding time for Harper to allow her creativity, autonomy, presentation skills, and adaptability to the culture to develop. It was a perfect example to me of the limitations placed on that sector of the workforce.

Making changes in this sector is nearly identical to that of the public education sector, but perhaps even more restricted, because doing anything other than what you are told to do is seen as insubordination and grounds for punitive actions or even dismissal. As you previously read in the chapter about power, and how power over someone is maintained, one of those methods is fear. If you are constantly living in fear of getting punished or potentially removed from the military for thinking outside of the box or attempting to fix a power dynamic, that would cause a major limitation on people wanting to take actions to correct that imbalance.

Self-Enthusiasts

The best part about this book is that no one can stop you from doing this work for yourself. There are no limitations on the work, the plans, or the investigation into empathy and power that you can provide for yourself. There is no limit to education or resources that a book or to which the internet can't provide you with access. The fact that there are no limitations means there is only one thing that can cause an issue. You. You are the only thing that can get in the way of discovering more about yourself and doing the work to determine if empathy and power are in balance in your own life at any given time. Sometimes this is the hardest part. Remember, we don't know what we don't know, and it is so very important to have a trusted friend, family member, or coworker who can hold you accountable or make you aware when you are preventing yourself from progress.

As you recall from the previous chapter, this work is a marathon and not a sprint. The work can sometimes be discouraging. After reading the book and feeling motivated to do this work and investigate, "Do I have an imbalance of empathy and power in my own life?" or deciding to work through it with a team, only to be met with a gigantic hurdle in your path, it may feel impossible. That is completely normal. I often say this to others: if the work to help people be better people was easy, it probably wasn't done right. This can be painful and frustrating work at times, but it is also exceedingly rewarding. I will use a question from a former executive coach that you can use if you find yourself at a blockade. "How can you find the space around the boulder?" If there are multiple boulders to move or get around, you may have to wait it out, or you may find a way to blast the boulder into smaller pieces. Either way, this is a journey.

After all of that, let's close with a little motivation.

CHAPTER 11:
Empathy and Power:
The Heart Work for the Hard Work

"If there is one thing we know for sure, it's that we know
nothing for sure." ~Socrates

One of my close friends always says, "I don't know nothin'!
I just read and keep trying stuff, and if it works, great!
If not, oh well. Do something else!"
"If things aren't adding up, start subtracting." ~Anonymous

"What you will allow will continue." ~Unknown

You could read this entire book, have a plan to start enacting it, and then life laughs at you and throws a monkey wrench into everything, simply because life is life! (My other favorite current quote: "Life be lifin'!")

Whether you are running into limitations or just need some encouragement that balancing empathy and power is possible, or you are simply learning to understand others and act accordingly, this chapter serves to be a motivation for your journey. I have often said that if it doesn't get hard or frustrating doing this work, you are probably not doing it correctly or to the best of your ability. Change is hard, but helping to shift mindsets in others is even more difficult, and it takes a special level of patience.

Let's shift back to some real-life stories. I will share some personal experiences from various parts of my life to demonstrate how balancing empathy, and power can happen at any point in your life, in any environment, whether planned or unexpected, whether personal or professional. It's important for you to see yourself in some of the shared stories so that you feel encouraged and hopeful for what is possible. It will show you that this is heart work for the hard work to be better humans, to develop a unified society and heal division.

Safety and Trust in School

During my time as an assistant principal, I was first placed in a school that was characterized by a high poverty rate. There were tragic car accidents, shootings, drugs, fights, and more in the surrounding community at any given time. Some may even be fearful to work in that environment, but I could not have found that time more rewarding, and I met some of the most caring people I have ever encountered. Most of the people who sent their kids to school were doing everything they could to survive and try to give their kids a better life than they had. Many of our seniors were first-time high school graduates in their families for generations, and this was in 2010.

In my third year in the building, I had found my stride and was connecting well with students, families, and community partners alike. So much so that I began to notice that the students counted on me as a trusted part of their circles, and they looked out for me often. I recall one day, I had to return to the school after hours because I had left something in my office that I had to retrieve before the weekend. It was late and it was dark. I was rarely worried when I was by the building, and I knew most of the people in the community, and they knew me.

On this one occasion, however, one of my students was standing across the street with a couple of friends whom I recognized from school. I waved and smiled and said, "Hey guys, don't you have some homework to do?" I chuckled, knowing that their reply would be a quick, "Not on a Friday night!" I was correct.

I laughed, and then one of the boys who was on the basketball team came up to me and said, "What are you doing out here by yourself?" I shared that I had left some things in the building that I needed for the weekend, and he said, "Yeah, this isn't the best time to be out here right now. Not tonight. We are gonna walk you to the door, and then we'll just stay here and walk you to your car when you come back out." I looked at him, and he was completely serious and had a look of concern on his face. He occasionally glanced to the left and right of the street as he spoke. His friends agreed as well. He also looked like he had some information about something that could potentially happen. I didn't inquire, which I learned is sometimes best not to do in the neighborhood. I just said, "Okay. But you all need to be safe too. Do I need to call our SRO to make sure you guys stay safe out here tonight?" (SRO stands for School Resource Officer and is our assigned school liaison to the city police department). He replied, "No, we will be okay."

Many of the kids were not too fond of the treatment of the police and often ignored their advice or commands, often to our dismay, choosing to be more respectful of our teachers and administrators. I always thought it was because they knew we took care of them and their families, and they truly didn't want to disappoint us. I didn't heed their warning, and when I got into the building, I did send a quick message to our two SROs to let them know and to ensure our kids were safe. They assured me they would send a patrol over. Knowledgeable and community oriented policing efforts go a long way in communities where trust is difficult.

When I exited the building, the students were right there by the front door. I wasn't surprised at all that they stayed, and I said, "Thanks for looking out for me, boys." They said, "It's all good," and even helped me carry a box to the car. I let them know that if they were concerned, they also needed to get off the street and head inside. Reluctantly, they said, "Oh, we will. We were just chillin' for a second." I smiled and told them I would see them on Monday. As I pulled away, I looked in my rearview mirror as they returned to their chill spot, and just then, I saw the police car turn the corner as I exited the street.

While this is not the main part of the story, I wanted to characterize the care and compassion that a majority of the students had for us and how well we knew all of them. I also wanted to shed light on the environment in which they lived, day in and day out. There was a constant priority on safety and survival, all while trying to just go to school.

On another normal school day morning, I had entered the building and did all of the normal things for my routine. I checked my emails, put my lunch away, grabbed something to drink from my office mini-fridge, and checked in with my principal. He was always there well before everyone else. After some of the office secretaries arrived, I turned on my walkie-talkie, which is how we all stayed in communication with each other throughout the day (like Morgan Freeman in *Lean on Me*), and I went to the top floor, where the high school teachers were getting their day started, also. I always walked through in the mornings as a check-in and to say hello.

One of the secretaries said my name on the walkie, and I responded. She asked me to come to her main office desk. I arrived at her desk. It was still well before most of the students would begin arriving and hanging out in front of the school before the first bell rang to head to class. She said, "There's a high school student outside and he is asking to speak to you. Well, he first asked for the principal, but I reminded him that while you are the assistant principal, you are the principal for the high school grade levels, and to speak with you first." I knew who the student was and wondered why he wouldn't come inside. I asked her that, and she said, "He's refusing to come in until he talks to only you." This was not uncommon. Many of the students only trusted a small circle of people, and often they did not speak to anyone outside of that circle.

I walked outside and I said, "Hey, sweet pea. What's going on?" He looked at me, and he looked scared and sad all at the same time. I saw his facial expression and I said, "What's the matter? Are you ok?" He said, "I'm okay… but like I'm sort of scared and don't know what to do and I don't want to get in trouble." I replied, "Okay. Tell me what's going on and I'll do my best to help." He said, "Please just let me tell you the entire story first." I agreed but mentioned that if it was a serious safety concern, I would have to alert someone in the building, depending on the issue.

He said, "So, you know there was that shooting where that man got killed last week just behind school?" and I nodded, "Mmhmm. Yeah, it's been tough on everyone. Did you know him?" He said, "Not really, but my dad did, and now my dad is really scared, and he really don't like it when I walk to school by myself in the dark," to which I replied, knowing how I'd feel as a parent in that situation, "I completely understand that. Did you need me to talk to your dad to see if we can get you a bus or someone to walk with so you aren't alone?" He said, "I can't ride the bus because I live too close, and usually my dad just drives me up here, but now he can't because of his job." I said, "Okay, well, we can figure that part out." He said, "And well, there's more. Today, I stopped at the store to get some chips and drink before school and when I opened my bookbag um, he put, um, a… weapon in my bookbag and it was wrapped in a note that told me to keep it for safety. It scared me, and I wanted to go back home, but I didn't have time because I was gonna be late for school, and I didn't want to get in trouble for being late, 'cause he'd be mad or think I did something or didn't wake up in time or something, and…"

As he started to get a little panicky. I said, "Okay, hold on. First, breathe and calm down. That won't help. Second, I am not going to ask what type of weapon, but you did the right thing by telling a school adult, someone who can keep you safe. I'm sorry your dad put you in that situation, although I…"

He interrupted me and said, "He's just scared, and he wanted me to be safe."

I said, "I understand that, but you know this is not allowed." I told him to wait there and that I was going to go get our principal and our school resource officer. That made him even more scared. He said, "I'm gonna get arrested?!" I said, "No, no, no, honey, I'm going to tell them what is happening and see if the officer can walk you back home and keep you safe and handle it that way." I instructed him to stay right by the door and not to move. I called for the principal and officer to meet me at the front of the building while I kept my eyes on the student, who was increasingly nervous by the minute.

When they arrived, I explained the situation. The officer calmly walked outside, shook the student's hand, and said, "Hey man, Ms. Hull told me what was going on. I'm gonna have to look in your backpack to see what's there and make sure we are all safe, and then we'll talk on the way to your house." He said, "Is my dad in trouble? Am I in trouble? I can't go to jail!" The officer said,

"No, man, you aren't going to go to jail, but we have to figure this out together. You did the right thing by telling us what was going on and being honest." The young man began to calm down, but was shaking a little bit. The officer looked at us and said, "I got it from here. I'll keep you posted." We nodded in thanks and went back inside. That entire conversation and scenario was all of about 10 minutes, and the school day resumed as normal.

I later learned that there was an unloaded gun in the boy's bookbag. I was not privy to what happened once the police got involved. Once things were reported to them, it was out of our hands as administrators since our purview was the school itself and school property. What I do know is that the student was the first in his family in three generations to graduate from high school and also the first to be accepted to college.

You may be wondering where the motivation or example is in this story. In that moment, he held a degree of power by having a weapon, and at one point so did I, as the administrator. I knew that my actions could potentially have led to panic, fear, and major consequences for the student for something that was out of his control. I had to have empathy for him and his father in that moment, even while the situation was somewhat tense. I had to have empathy for the father who was terrified of his son being fatally wounded just walking to school in the morning and not knowing how to keep him safe. I also had to have empathy for the students and people in the building, knowing that my power and responsibility were centered on safety of the school population. However, I had to maintain my power as the adult and administrator in that position, ensure no one was hurt, and keep a weapon out of our school.

In balancing empathy and power, sometimes the solution is the approach *and* the response. Sometimes the solution is to recognize in that moment how your own empathy and power can have a lasting effect on someone else's life. You have the ability to control those moments for yourself. You have the ability to help others practice how to do that with the knowledge you have gained in this book and helping others to see that showing empathy does not mean losing power, yet it means maintaining it at the right level for the right situations and knowing when to turn the dial up or down on either side of the empathy and power continuum.

Mentoring And Sponsorship — A Corporate Example

In one of my roles as a corporate executive working closely with the senior leadership on the human resources team, I was tasked with identifying trends among various groups of employees in the business based on the results from our annual engagement survey. This survey asks a variety of questions about how people feel at work, how they engage with their work, their role, their manager, and their overall feeling about the company as well. They are also given the opportunity to comment freely if they have additional thoughts about their experience.

In the fall of 2023, as a team, we began to identify more and more comments that were centered around employees feeling left behind, disconnected from senior leaders, and that there weren't enough opportunities for employees on the frontline to gain access to various programs. Inside the business, we had several leadership programs built for leaders and executive leaders, but there were not many programs invested in helping those on the frontline grow in their skills or develop their professional careers. We were hearing comments like, "the senior leaders have no idea what it's like for us," or "it would be nice to have something that helps us develop or gain more leadership skills." We also noticed engagement scores beginning to trend down for those in positions that would be considered "entry level" or those who had less tenure in the business.

My team had the opportunity to also engage in some discussions with some of our frontline and entry-level employees, and the sentiments were the same. They felt disconnected from our senior leaders, and they also felt like the senior leaders were disconnected from their experiences as well. They began to provide examples of times when different decisions could have been considered if there were more open dialogue about the day-to-day life of a frontline associate in different parts of the business. I started to realize that there were two major concerns: training and a human disconnect because of how levels and teams were structured. Now, you can also identify that this was a power and empathy imbalance as well because the organizational structure kept a distance between those at the top senior leadership levels and those in the entry level positions. Limiting education and connection to others, as you read in the chapters above, are two ways to maintain an imbalance in power structures and increase the imbalance between empathy and power.

We are a small team, so the time investment we had to make was more significant. As we centered on the root cause of this imbalance, we decided the best way to solve it was to create a meaningful mentoring and sponsorship program. Three of us on the team had the opportunity to go to a great conference earlier that year and attended a session about how to increase diverse representation in senior levels of leadership. The presentation centered on the importance of not just mentoring but sponsoring those who may not have the networks or access to the right networks within a company, in order to learn more or simply have their work accomplishments elevated to the right people. I spoke about the research that we used for the matching portion of the program within Chapter 2 about empathy. It is the seven pillars of connectivity.

While I spoke about the success rate of the matching for this program being centered around this research previously, what is even more critical to point out is that when mentoring programs are unsuccessful, it is because the matching is forced, at random, or done without intentional effort to ensure a positive relationship can develop. On our team, we also kept the cohort small. In order to build a program that had meaningful components, and due to our own capacity, we kept the cohort to a maximum of 20 pairs. We sought nominations and interest from across the business in all departments.

Our mentors were at a certain level of leadership, ranging from Senior Managers all the way to C-suite executives, and our mentees were all in frontline or entry level positions that had not yet reached levels of leadership within the organization. The entry level and frontline parts of the organization are the most diverse in their interests, their demographics, their tenure in the business and more. Throughout the program, participants raved about the connection, the perspective they were gathering from both sides, and how it has shifted the direction of their careers. Some made shifts to other departments, some were promoted, and our mentors discussed how they had forgotten what the day-to-day was like for a frontline employee because it had been so long since they faced that every day themselves. In turn, the mentors became permanent fixtures in the lives of their mentees and acted as sponsors to assist them in their career journeys by elevating their work and their goals to other leaders in the organization.

It didn't take long for the word about the opportunity that the program had given to the participants to spread, and it started shifting the narrative. We found that the solution for disconnect and training was to create a meaningful experience for relationships to develop between people who would not have normally had that experience. We utilized assessments, online coaching courses, and our own meeting platform to encourage regular contact, and the program concluded with a presentation for the participants to demonstrate what they accomplished during their structured time together.

The imbalance in empathy and power shifted as they learned more about each other. Human connection and the willingness to learn about someone else, coupled with service, is one of the greatest ways to correct an imbalance between empathy and power.

This example is not meant to boast about a phenomenal program, but it does show that the solutions to balancing empathy and power are usually related to allowing for dialogue and providing perspective or access to groups of people that may not naturally connect on their own. Human connection is powerful when that connection is for the purpose of balancing power rather than maintaining control over another. In this case, those who held more power as a result of their leadership status in the business had been so far removed from the frontline experience that they did not even realize or know what they didn't know. It's just like the dead bush scenario. Reminding others and giving them those realities makes it tangible and visible. You have the ability to do this with the imbalances you may encounter. It takes time. The build and execution of this program took almost a full fiscal year. If we can do it, so can you!

The Yes Girl – An Individual Example

I call myself a recovered people pleaser. Growing up, I cared a LOT about what other people thought of me. I was always fearful of saying or doing something that would make someone not like me. I never said no and often found myself trying to fix or adjust myself to accommodate what others may want to do rather than what I really wanted to do myself. I was a yes girl.

I discussed giving power away "ad nauseam" in Chapter 5, so I won't belabor the point here in this short story. You have also seen an example of it in my discussion of losing my relationship with the outdoor environment. This is a bit different than that, however, because what I found myself doing all the way up to my adult life was constantly catering to what others wanted. I was putting others before myself to an extreme. I was giving my power away to others because my levels of empathy were so high and toxic that I was allowing others to control my emotions, my thoughts, and what essentially made me happy. I had always viewed doing things for myself and not bending over backwards to be present for and help others in whatever capacity was needed as selfish. I did not realize I was slowly torturing myself.

One day, I went to a self-help retreat of sorts, and slowly they taught us strategies to put ourselves first. I had gone through a personal tragedy and was finding it difficult to regain my own power and emotional strength. We went through intense emotional exercises and reached back into different parts of our lives to figure out what led us to what was causing us a source of pain. The one exercise I remember most was visualizing going back into your childhood home and imagining how it felt to walk through the door. They asked what we saw, what sparked our memories the most. Not everyone had the safe and loving childhood home that I had, so for some, this exercise was triggering, but necessary to uncover their root cause of pain and learn how to walk through it. What I discovered was that it was the last time I felt completely safe and supported by others to be whatever I wanted to be in life without fear of rejection and the fear of being alone. Since leaving home, something had changed, and I had developed a fear of being rejected or alone if I told anyone, "no." It was at that precise moment that I started to learn how to gain my own power back and give myself permission to create that space for myself.

I opened the chapter with a few quotes, and the one that stood out as the starting point for me to start saying no was "when things aren't adding up, start subtracting." There were friendships I had to sever, there were relationships that struggled because of how I changed my approach to them, there were jobs I was no longer willing to do, and people I had to say no to more often. It was really difficult to work through that and gain the confidence that I have now. But slowly, I reclaimed some of my power in my life and found a healthy way to use empathy to benefit self.

Remember, I am not cured from being a people pleaser, I am a recovered people pleaser and there are times that I still catch myself doing too much for others before myself and to my detriment. It is so very important to work every day towards the balance of empathy and power not just for our world, our country, our communities and our jobs, but for ourselves.

Investigating and realizing that the imbalance of empathy and power is at the root of division in our society and in ourselves is one of the most impactful discoveries of my life. We have the ability to heal our nation's divides if we learn to balance the empathy and power continuum. Having the confidence to introduce a concept to the world in a way that has not been presented in this fashion is a bold and empowering act. It is with the sole intent of wanting to see all of us unify rather than divide. It is with the desire that we can create a country (or world) that respects the idea that two opinions can exist at the same time and that rather than exerting authority and demanding that only one opinion is right or wrong, we learn to listen and consider all sides to create a best third option. It is with pure hope that everyone will read and learn that having power is not right or wrong, nor does having empathy for others that we know or don't know make us weaker. We can interact with these forces and actions to unify rather than divide our communities. A mentor of mine often says to others, "The work has to be in you to come through you." This book, these solutions, and the work you will do are all methods to help the concept be instilled within you. Rediscovering your inner power, your empathy, and guiding change for others so that it may come through you to develop unity and to heal divides is purpose of this book.

Begin within.

Learn and locate.

Unify and build.

Enact and nurture.

Be the example and create the blueprint for a more unified society at a time that we need it most.

To balance empathy and power will be the greatest test of our ability to succeed as a unified people.

Appendix A:
Demonstrating Empathy
in Childhood and Adolescence

Young Children

I had the pleasure of watching my mom teach children as young as three how to be empathetic. My mom was a Montessori preschool teacher. This woman, my mother, was obsessed with the concept of Montessori education and with Maria Montessori herself. If you are unfamiliar, Maria Montessori was an Italian physician, inventor, and innovator, and she developed an educational philosophy that used the physical, social, and psychological development of children as tools for learning. It sounds fancy, but my mom explained it as "learning as play." Children learn at exceptional rates through guided learning and by allowing them to learn through various intentional activities and out in the environment itself. The world becomes their classroom.

Needless to say, my sister and I both attended Montessori preschool and elementary school, and my mom passed that tradition down as my two sons and niece have all been enrolled in a Montessori school in their lives. One of the concepts that is incorporated into the Montessori instructional philosophy is learning from peers, and to do so, respect and collaboration are key measures of success regardless of age. For example, at an early age in Montessori education, students are paired together to teach concepts to one another if one student has mastered a concept. In this way, the classroom places the teacher or instructor in the position of facilitator of learning rather than the authority of learning. The student becomes the teacher, and every student typically has the opportunity to do so. The instructional design places multiple age groups in one classroom; for this reason, students work together, collaborate, and respect what they can learn from their peers.

Every now and then, I would get the opportunity to be in the classroom with my mom when she taught, and I remember how she carefully handled the little ones, some of them just fresh off of potty training (one of the exact reasons why I did not teach that age). In my observations of her and of the children, I noticed she never treated them like babies; she taught them responsibility for themselves and care and compassion for each other and the materials. After a little while, they look like little mini adults washing dishes, tracing letters, writing, and teaching their friends how to wash vegetables or button and zip shirts.

I recall one time, my mom was on the floor sitting with her legs folded under her, or "criss-cross applesauce" (which is customary in these classrooms to get on the level of the child), and a group of students in kindergarten were in the reading corner. One little girl seemed to be frustrated, and she threw the book on the floor, had a scowl on her face, and crossed her arms. One of the male students looked at her and could sense her anger. I heard him say, "It's okay, Destiny. It was hard for me, too. I can read with you to help you." The little girl's face softened, and she looked at him, looked at my mom across the room, then looked at the book. Slowly she unfolded her arms and picked up the book and put the book in *his* lap. It was clear she was accepting help from him but on her terms. He picked it up from his lap and started reading, and I could see him pointing to words in the book with his finger. At first, she was listening, and then she put one hand on the book to pull it closer to her lap, and soon she was holding the book in her lap again. That little boy, at the ripe age of five, successfully used empathy by understanding what she was feeling, coupled it with compassion, and helped Destiny realize her own potential.

This story reveals an important lesson about empathy. Empathy does not have to be as complicated or involve exceptional overthinking, as adults tend to do. Empathy can also be so simple that a four-year-old child can demonstrate it. My mom had a poster that read, "All I need to know I learned in kindergarten," and the little boy who helped Destiny is an example. Someone does not have to use words to show empathy towards another. Empathy can be quite simple. It can be an act of togetherness, of presence, and of living in someone else's moment with them. Empathy is not judgmental or rushed, and it also does not mean that those receiving it do not learn for themselves. By being by someone's side, we help them learn better.

Adolescence and the Teen Years

At some point, as a child begins to mature and their brains continue development, they begin to learn reason, logic, and more complex emotions. The life that used to be simple becomes more difficult to navigate amidst these changes. As children grow into adolescents, their brains take in enormous amounts of information that form into stored memories, lessons, and rules. The patterns, beliefs, and internal thoughts that they have at this age are mainly formed from experiences in various environments depending on their own life circumstances. These adolescents could be wealthy or in financial need. They could live in a place where cars are a necessary part of life or in a busy city where walking is required. They could attend church regularly or play sports.

Most adolescents collect information at school both intellectually and socially. There is a multitude of information that they must process and make sense of for themselves. It is a lot to handle, which is why these middle adolescent years are so difficult for so many kids.

Somewhere in this journey, empathy gets to be a bit less natural for some teens because they may feel weird showing empathy. You see, empathy requires someone to be vulnerable in order to effectively show it. At this stage, their brains are taking in information faster than they can interpret it, their bodies are changing, their emotions are all over the place, and they are trying to figure out whom they can trust, who their friends will be, and most importantly, who they want to be. It is difficult to then expose the parts of themselves that they are unsure of to someone else in an empathetic moment. In addition, at this age they are also layering in the importance of the social circle. Ensuring that one is fitting in, making friends, or finding people who align with the same thoughts and feelings as them, all while you are figuring out who they are, and *then* attempting to be empathetic? Whew! That is a really hard thing to do. It's understandable if our adolescents and teens struggle to show empathy, especially if they aren't used to receiving it. It is equally important for us to show empathy to our teens, knowing that they are going through these tough developmental years.

I am the mom of two teen boys who are seventeen and fourteen at the time of publication. If anyone has ever said that boys aren't emotional, it's a lie. I would argue that boys are usually more emotional than women but are just not granted social permission to express them in the way they should in order to be healthy. I try to teach my boys that emotion is important and when they feel something, rather than hold it in, they should find a safe place (even if it isn't with me) to express that emotion. Expressing emotion or having emotional regularity is a part of empathy. Having said that, they are very kind kids. I am biased on this one like most parents, but I have gotten compliments from several adults, unprompted, that they are kind and thoughtful kids. I'm grateful for that, but they are still teenagers. There have been moments when they have had to relearn how to be empathetic.

My oldest went through a bit of a medical scare at the start of his Junior year of high school, and it took an emotional toll on all of us for a bit as we cared for him until he returned to his normal self. In that span of time, I also observed my youngest son shift attention away from himself. I am always in awe of my youngest son's self-confidence. It isn't boastful or self-serving or egotistical in a negative way, yet it's just a clear confidence and trust in oneself. He was born with it. Typically, he does like attention and enjoys being at the center as an extrovert. But, when this incident occurred, I saw a visible shift in how he directed his attention in these important moments. It was kind, thoughtful, and it was obvious that he was taking other people's emotions and experiences to heart.

After the dust had settled with the scare, and all of our lives had resumed some normalcy, I was driving my youngest home from middle school, and he said, "Mom, I really think what Dre went through helped me too." I replied, "Oh yea? How so?" And he said, "Well, we were at lunch today, and one of my friends was telling this story about a family member who was really sick. I don't know what was wrong with their family, but he said he was nervous to be around them because he didn't want to do the wrong thing or say the wrong thing. And I told him 'I know what you mean, bruh. I just went through that too,' but then I told him that it's scary at first but the more you are around them and just be yourself, the better the other person will feel too and then you won't be nervous anymore." And because I, as the mom, have to "act cool" in these moments so I don't ruin them with my proud mommy tears, I replied, "That's good bub. Really good. What did he say?" And in normal teen fashion, he replied, "He just said, 'yeah,' and we started talking about something else. But it made me realize that I kind of understand people better when they say their family is going through stuff."

My son's lesson in empathy was brought to him through life experience. Sometimes, even in times of great confusion, information overload, and uncertainty, it is still possible to be empathetic to another person. Empathy is situational, meaning there will be situations in which you are able to show more empathy because you can directly relate to a person's experiences, and there will be times when you can't. It is in those moments that bravery, courage, and vulnerability are required so that we can tap into the feelings we had in those experiences and use them to help be there for someone else. Someone at any age can do this, and this story is an example.

Acknowledgments

There is no possible way this book would have happened without the involvement of several people. First and foremost, I have to thank my parents. Their life lessons and example have shaped the stories in this book and provided a foundation on which I am able to live as a parent, professional and person in the world. Without my mom forcing us to read constantly in the summer and watching her excel as an adult with kids, I would not have the inner strength to do the same. Arthur and Carmen are the GOATS.

Next, thank you to my family and all of my friends who have become family! Andre and Andrew, you are the light of my life. You were patient and understanding every time I had to step away from our time together to write, review, or edit the book or travel for work. Mom guilt is real, but you boys are my inspiration and motivation to never stop. To my sister, Betty and niece Grace, thank you for all of your support as I worked through this year and managed all that occurred in the course of the year of writing and getting the book published. We are all we have sometimes and the boys and I love you! To my Uncle, Aunt and Cousins in my future Cali home: Uncle Arnold for waiting for me at the bottom of the airport escalator every time I arrive, Aunt Susan for being my largest cheerleader for the world to see, Tony for being my big bro cousin and lifetime protector, Bijan for the girls nights, Danny for your groundbreaking art that I get to share after tattoo therapy and Nate for your support, football and baseball banter! I need all of you, and I'm so very grateful!

To all of my friends that are sisters who were present to read my first words written, listened to me talk about it over and over again, supported, who gave me actual stories, a chapter title, and content, and made time to force me to step away and get some space from the writing process: Bianca, Shantel, Kim, Rashida, Natalie, Autumn, Shayna, and every other person that has supported me along the way from the various parts of my world. Thank you! Extra thanks to Bianca for being a proofreader when I needed you! And extra thanks to Shantel for being the muse for Chapter 7!

The co-parenting relationship I have built with my boy's Dad, Scott, and their Step-Mom Onaney has also made this book possible as well as the support of the kids grandparents: Robin and Carol. It doesn't have to be perfect to work, and it hasn't always been easy or without conflict or obstacles, but we are doing it and the boys are thriving. I'm appreciative of your partnership during the times I've had to step out of town and away to finish the book on top of all of the work things. We remain Team Boys!

I had the idea and the vision, but to get it all down and actually develop the story and the concept with real words, it would have been a project of nothingness without Joy Eggerichs and Amelia Graves from Punchline Agency, Larissa Conte, founder and owner of Wayfinding, Seramount, a subsidiary of EAB and its consultants for their generosity that led to my knowledge of the authors of *Navigating Polarities* and consultants at Andiron. Joy and Amelia, thank you for your guidance, your edits, and questions that pushed this book way further than I ever thought it could go with content. Larissa, ditto the nothingness that this book would be without you and your work. Not only did you help develop me as a person and a professional in great times and in difficult ones, but your research on the power landscapes are foundational for the book, not surprisingly growing from the roots of our work together, like the roots of a tree, which has a clear meaning for me. Thank you!

Thanks to my entire Punchline book cohort! Your support from here to England has been unwavering and kind. Thanks to Valarie McCarthy for your professional and personal friendship and for being a support to this book journey. You are an amazing writer, and I'm grateful to have had your help in proofreading this work. Steph Bradford, you were the first person to coach me into being a great educator. Thank you for investing in me and for taking the time to help this book cross the finish line! Karen Crone, you are the reason I am able to write this with knowledge of the corporate sector because you took a chance on this former high school assistant principal and gave me the autonomy and trust to build an entire department for a private corporate business. I'm appreciative of your continued investment in my growth and journey. Thank you to Tommie Lewis, a mentor and the first person to acknowledge that I had a gift outside of the educational sphere. You were the first person to respond, "Write it! Write it now!" back in 2018 when I mentioned wanting to write a book. Instead of competition, you encouraged me and that meant everything at that time professionally!

Thanks to all of my high school English teachers, Betsy Shank for teaching me the art of including my voice in writing and public speaking skills, and Sharon Draper, for listening to me talk about writing about a book for years now and continuing to provide guidance and resources even as you continue your journey as an award-winning author and movie contributor. To my Walnut Hills High School family: "Sursum Ad Summum." The legacy of excellence continues. Thank you to Jeff Brokamp for your mentorship through my teaching and administrative years. I am grateful for your examples of how to lead when others perceive you differently than what you are capable of accomplishing. Thanks to all of my OU family for being there along the way, and to those of you who I am closer to who have listened, sometimes daily, offered support, encouragement, and more, I am grateful. Thank you to all of my Sorors of Delta Sigma Theta Sorority, Inc., and more specifically, Epsilon Iota Chapter and Greater Cincinnati Alumnae Chapter. The bonds we have created are eternal and lifelong, and I will always hold every one of you near and dear to my soul. AOML always! OO-OOP my Sorors! Thank you to all of my sports friends and families that have also played a part in listening to me jabber on the sides of baseball and football fields as well as help me laugh about the journey! Hotel room lobbies won't ever be prepared for us!

Thank you to all of those that have endorsed the book and have played a role in promoting the book: Swiftbook Marketing, Ricardo Grant, Alex Meacham, Dustin Woods, Claudia Abercrumbie, Deje'a Miller "Foodies with a Cutie," Ashley Ferguson (amazing children's book author, please check her out), and anyone else my middle-aged brain is leaving out. I am so grateful for you!

To my Pike family! You truly have no idea what it means to have this place in my life. It has sustained me through so many tough times and celebrations in the good times! There have been a few that have been there from the beginning and are still here as friends! I would be remiss not to mention you as you have been a part of my life for the last 13 years. I can't wait to celebrate this book with you!

There are several that have chosen not to be named individually, but late-night rants over text or random IG reels to get my mind off of the craziness and more, you know who you are and thank you!

On behalf of people everywhere, I say thank you to those who have dedicated their lives to the unity of human relationships instead of the separation and isolation of people. It is not easy work to do when we live in a world that is fueled by the accumulation of money and power rather than using money and power to promote more balance and harmony in our communities across America and the world.

I have no idea how pervasive this work will become, but what I do know is that I did it in spite of every obstacle that was thrown in my path. I created a legacy for my family and my ancestors by becoming a published author. I am grateful to anyone I have not mentioned who has played a role in my life.

I won't stop.

[1] "Brene Brown on Empathy." RSA Shorts, voice by Dr. Brene Brown, animation by Katy Davis, December 10, 2013, YouTube, https://www.youtube.com/watch?v=1Evwgu369Jw.

[2] Susane Lanzoni, Empathy: A History (Yale University Press, 2018), 8-9.

[3] "Empathy" Merriam-Webster, accessed July 10, 2025, https://www.merriam-webster.com/dictionary/empathy.

[4] "Brene Brown on Empathy." RSA Shorts, voice by Dr. Brene Brown, animation by Katy Davis, December 10, 2013, YouTube, https://www.youtube.com/watch?v=1Evwgu369Jw.

[5] Queen Charlotte, season 1, episode 1, "Queen to Be," written by Shonda Rhimes, directed by Tom Verica, aired May 4, 2023, on Netflix.

[6] Jean Decety, "The Neurodevelopment of Empathy in Humans," Developmental Neuroscience 32, no. 4 (January 1, 2010): 257–67, https://doi.org/10.1159/000317771.

[7] "Increasing Diversity Among Senior Leadership." Seramount, October 2022, accessed on July 10, 2025, https://seramount.com/research/increasing-diversity-among-senior-leadership/

[8] Cheryl Wold, Andria Moon, Anna Schwan, Alan Neville, and Janeen Outka."The Importance of Pairings in Mentorship Programs." Critical Questions in Educations 14, no. 2 (2023), https://files.eric.ed.gov/fulltext/EJ1382022.pdf; Keagan McMahon, "Maximizing Potential: The Power of the Right Mentor Match." Together: An Absorb Company, May 21, 2024, accessed July 10, 2025, https://www.togetherplatform.com/blog/maximizing-potential-the-power-of-the-right-mentor-match.

[9] "Blackface: The Birth of An American Stereotype." National Museum of African American History and Culture accessed July 10, 2025, https://nmaahc.si.edu/explore/stories/black-face-birth-american-stereotype.

[10] Afrian Florido, Jonaki Mehta, and Patrick Jarenwattananon, "Many Know How George Floyd Died. A New Biography Reveals How He Lived." NPR, May 18, 2022, https://www.npr.org/2022/05/18/1099585400/george-floyd-biography-book.

[11] Understanding Unconscious Bias." School of Public Health, Harvard Longwood Campus. https://content.sph.harvard.edu/wwwhsph/sites/2597/2022/06/Types-of-Bias-Ways-to-Manage-Bias_HANDOUT-1.pdf.

[12] "Radical Empathy | Terri Givens," Terri Givens, July 1, 2025, https://www.terrigivens.com/radicalempathy/.

[13] Abramson, Ashley. "Cultivating Empathy: Psychologists' Research Offers Insight Into Why It's So Important to Practice the 'Right' Kind of Empathy, and How to Grow Those Skills." American Psychological Association, 52, no. 8 (2021), https://www.apa.org/monitor/2021/11/feature-cultivating-empathy.

[14] Andrew R. Todd, Galen V. Bodenhausen, Jennifer A. Richeson, and Adam D. Galinsky. "Perspective Taking Combats Automatic Expressions of Racial Bias." Journal of Personality and Social Psychology, 100, no. 6, 1027-2042, https://doi.org/10.1037/a0022308.

[15] Jakob Franzen, "Seven Benefits When You Lead With Empathy." Forbes, February 15, 2023. https://www.forbes.com/councils/forbescoachescouncil/2023/02/15/seven-benefits-when-you-lead-with-empathy/.

[16] "Reciprocity in Relationships: 3 Types of Reciprocity." MasterClass, May 5, 2022. https://www.masterclass.com/articles/reciprocity-in-relationships.

[17] "Power," Dictionary, accessed July 10, 2025, https://www.dictionary.com/browse/power.

[18] Larissa Conte, "Wayfinding," 2024, https://www.wayfinding.io/.

[19] Larissa Conte, "Power," 2023, https://www.wayfinding.io/power-up.

[20] Larissa Conte, "Wayfinding," 2024, https://www.wayfinding.io/.

[21] Larissa Conte, "Power," 2023, https://www.wayfinding.io/power-up.

[22] The Empire Strikes Back, directed by Steven Spielberg (20th Century Fox, 1980), https://www.imdb.com/title/tt0080684/.

[23] Warfare History Network, "The Madman of the Mountain: Adolf Hitler's Personal Life - Warfare History Network," June 20, 2025, https://warfarehistorynetwork.com/article/the-madman-of-the-mountain-adolf-hitlers-personal-life/.

[24] Center for Substance Abuse Treatment, "Understanding the Impact of Trauma," Trauma-Informed Care in Behavioral Health Services - NCBI Bookshelf, 2014, https://www.ncbi.nlm.nih.gov/books/NBK207191/.

[25] Kelsie Smith Hayduk, "Researchers Reveal How Trauma Changes the Brain," URMC Newsroom, June 13, 2023, https://www.urmc.rochester.edu/news/publications/neuroscience/researchers-reveal-how-trauma-changes-the-brain.

[26] Malory Plummer and Annie Cossins, "The Cycle of Abuse: When Victims Become Offenders," Trauma Violence & Abuse 19, no. 3 (July 19, 2016): 296–298, https://doi.org/10.1177/1524838016659487.

[27] Kathryn Kvas, "Is It Anxiety, or Is a Tiger Trying to Kill You?" The New Yorker, December 31, 2024, https://www.newyorker.com/humor/shouts-murmurs/is-it-anxiety-or-is-a-tiger-trying-to-kill-you#:~:text=To%20help%20patients%20understand%20anxiety,and%20loss%20of%20bowel%20control.

[28] "The Science of Drug Use: A Resource for the Justice Sector | National Institute on Drug Abuse," National Institute on Drug Abuse, November 22, 2023, https://nida.nih.gov/research-topics/criminal-justice/science-drug-use-resource-justice-sector.

[29] Sean Peek, "Why Does Power Abuse Persist?," business.com, June 2, 2025, https://www.business.com/articles/psychology-of-power-abuse/.

[30] Tobore Onojighofia Tobore, "On Power and Its Corrupting Effects: The Effects of Power on Human Behavior and the Limits of Accountability Systems," Communicative & Integrative Biology 16, no. 1 (August 24, 2023), https://doi.org/10.1080/19420889.2023.2246793.

[31] "Amygdala," Cleveland Clinic, March 11, 2023, https://my.clevelandclinic.org/health/body/24894-amygdala.

[32] "Cerebral Cortex," Cleveland Clinic, May 23, 2022, https://my.clevelandclinic.org/health/articles/23073-cerebral-cortex.

[33] FOX Soul, "Kimberly Latrice Jones on Her Viral 'Monopoly' Video | the Tammi Mac Late Show," June 14, 2020, https://www.youtube.com/watch?v=4FsZLImSL4s.

[34] Focus 3, "Leadership Development and Culture Training Systems | Focus 3," February 17, 2025, https://focus3.com/systems/.

[35] Don Miguel Ruiz, The Four Agreements : A Practical Guide to Personal Freedom, 2011, https://ci.nii.ac.jp/ncid/BA83191420.

[36] Nedra Glover Tawwab, Set Boundaries, Find Peace: A Guide to Reclaiming Yourself (Penguin, 2021).

[37] Brian Emerson and Kelly Lewis, Navigating Polarities: Using Both/and Thinking to Lead Transformation (Paradoxical Press, 2019).

[38] Barry Johnson, PhD, "Polarity Management: A Summary Introduction," Polarity Management Associates, May 2005, https://rise-leaders.com/wp-content/uploads/2019/07/Polarity-Management-Summary-Introduction.pdf.

[39] Stephen Marsar, "Rules of Engagement," book-chapter, Fire Officer I, n.d., https://www.co.monmouth.nj.us/documents/23/ch16_rules%20of%20engagement_foi.pdf.

[40] School Daze, directed by Spike Lee (40 Acres and a Mule Filmworks, 1988), https://www.imdb.com/title/tt0096054/.

[41] Herrmann, "Understanding Whole Brain® Thinking," https://www.thinkherrmann.com/why-herrmann.

[42] Jonathan Jarry, M. Sc., "An Ancient Memory Technique Still Puzzles Scientists," McGill Office for Science and Society, January 12, 2024, https://research.wou.edu/c.php?g=551307&p=3785490.

[43] Gallup, Inc., "Create a Culture That Inspires People," Gallup.com, March 17, 2018, https://www.gallup.com/workplace/229832/culture.aspx.

[44] NYC Public Schools Organizational Chart," n.d., https://pwsblobprd.schools.nyc/prd-pws/docs/default-source/default-document-library/nycps-organizational-chart-dec-2024.pdf?s-fvrsn=2d8181ec_2.

Figure 1. "Wayfinding Power Landscape," Wayfinding, 2023, https://www.wayfinding.io/

Figure 2: "Shadow Powers ," Wayfinding, 2023, https://www.wayfinding.io/

About the Author

Amy E. Hull, M.Ed., has broken barriers and transformed corporate strategy into measurable results that have garnered national recognition. Under her leadership, several organizations in multiple sectors have achieved systemic change and growth in human relationships, engagement, and understanding. Hull has received several awards from a variety of organizations for her professional accomplishments, including the Northern Kentucky Chamber of Commerce, Brandon Hall HCM Excellence, Top Workplaces Energage, Cincinnati USA Regional Chamber, HRO Today International, and was featured on the cover of HR Futures Magazine. During her 17 years in education, she was featured in the Amazon Prime documentary, Oyler School (2013), for her work alongside the administration and staff in a poverty-stricken community.

Amy holds a B.S. in Biology from Ohio University and two M.Ed. degrees in Education and Administration from Xavier University and the University of Cincinnati. She founded and owns Hull Humanity Ventures, LLC, and is represented by APB Speakers Bureau. Civically, Amy is an active member of Delta Sigma Theta Sorority, Inc., serves on the Executive Leadership team for Go Red for Women Cincinnati, a strong supporter of Girls Health Period and lifetime member of NAAHR, Inc.

Amy is proud to be the mom to her two incredible sons, enjoys traveling, loves dogs, music, watching football, tennis, and baseball. She is devoted to her life's work of education, connecting people across the mosaic of humanity and creating unity in our world.